بسم الله الرحمن الرحيم

# LET'S LEARN OUR ISLAM

## HARUN YAHYA

Ta-Ha Publishers Ltd.
I Wynne Road London SW9 OBB

# About The Author

Now writing under the pen-name of HARUN YAHYA, he was born in Ankara in 1956. Having completed his primary and secondary education in Ankara, he studied arts at Istanbul's Mimar Sinan University and philosophy at Istanbul University. Since the 1980s, he has published many books on political, scientific, and faith-related issues. Harun Yahya is well-known as the author of important works disclosing the imposture of evolutionists, their invalid claims, and the dark liaisons between Darwinism and such bloody ideologies as fascism and communism.

His pen-name is a composite of the names *Harun* (Aaron) and *Yahya* (John), in memory of the two esteemed Prophets who fought against their people's lack of faith. The Prophet's seal on the his books' covers is symbolic and is linked to the their contents. It represents the Qur'an (the final scripture) and the Prophet Muhammad (peace be upon him), last of the prophets. Under the guidance of the Qur'an and the Sunnah (teachings of the Prophet), the author makes it his purpose to disprove each fundamental tenet of godless ideologies and to have the "last word," so as to completely silence the objections raised against religion. He uses the seal of the final Prophet, who attained ultimate wisdom and moral perfection, as a sign of his intention to offer the last word.

All of Harun Yahya's works share one single goal: to convey the Qur'an's message, encourage readers to consider basic faith-related issues such as Allah's Existence and Unity and the hereafter; and to expose godless systems' feeble foundations and perverted ideologies.

Harun Yahya enjoys a wide readership in many countries, from India to America, England to Indonesia, Poland to Bosnia, and Spain to Brazil. Some of his books are available in English, French, German, Spanish, Italian, Portuguese, Urdu, Arabic, Albanian, Russian, Serbo-Croat (Bosnian), Polish, Malay, Uygur Turkish, and Indonesian.

Greatly appreciated all around the world, these works have been instrumental in many people recovering faith in Allah and gaining deeper insights into their faith. His books' wisdom and sincerity, together with a distinct style that's easy to understand, directly affect anyone who reads them. Those who seriously consider these books, can no longer advocate atheism or any other perverted ideology or materialistic philosophy, since these books are characterized by rapid effectiveness, definite results, and irrefutability. Even if they continue to do so, it will be only a sentimental insistence, since these books refute such ideologies from their very foundations. All contemporary movements of denial are now ideologically defeated, thanks to the books written by Harun Yahya.

This is no doubt a result of the Qur'an's wisdom and lucidity. The author modestly intends to serve as a means in humanity's search for Allah's right path. No material gain is sought in the publication of these works.

Those who encourage others to read these books, to open their minds and hearts and guide them to become more devoted servants of Allah, render an invaluable service.

Meanwhile, it would only be a waste of time and energy to propagate other books that create confusion in people's minds, lead them into ideological chaos, and that clearly have no strong and precise effects in removing the doubts in people's hearts, as also verified from previous experience. It is impossible for books devised to emphasize the author's literary power rather than the noble goal of saving people from loss of faith, to have such a great effect. Those who doubt this can readily see that the sole aim of Harun Yahya's books is to overcome disbelief and to disseminate the Qur'an's moral values. The success and impact of this service are manifested in the readers' conviction.

One point should be kept in mind: The main reason for the continuing cruelty, conflict, and other ordeals endured by the vast majority of people is the ideological prevalence of disbelief. This can be ended only with the ideological defeat of disbelief and by conveying the wonders of creation and Qur'anic morality so that people can live by it. Considering the state of the world today, leading into a downward spiral of violence, corruption and conflict, clearly this service must be provided speedily and effectively, or it may be too late.

In this effort, the books of Harun Yahya assume a leading role. By the will of Allah, these books will be a means through which people in the twentyfirst century will attain the peace, justice, and happiness promised in the Qur'an.

# To The Reader

In all the books by the author, faith-related issues are explained in the light of the Qur'anic verses and people are invited to learn Allah's words and to live by them. All the subjects that concern Allah's verses are explained in such a way as to leave no room for doubt or question marks in the reader's mind. The sincere, plain and fluent style employed ensures that everyone of every age and from every social group can easily understand the books. This effective and lucid narrative makes it possible to read them in a single sitting. Even those who rigorously reject spirituality are influenced by the facts recounted in these books and cannot refute the truthfulness of their contents.

This book and all the other works of the author can be read individually or discussed in a group at a time of conversation. Those readers who are willing to profit from the books will find discussion very useful in the sense that they will be able to relate their own reflections and experiences to one another.

In addition, it will be a great service to the religion to contribute to the presentation and reading of these books, which are written solely for the good pleasure of Allah. All the books of the author are extremely convincing. For this reason, for those who want to communicate the religion to other people, one of the most effective methods is to encourage them to read these books.

It is hoped that the reader will take time to look through the review of other books on the final pages of the book, and appreciate the rich source of material on faith-related issues, which are very useful and a pleasure to read.

In these books, you will not find, as in some other books, the personal views of the author, explanations based on dubious sources, styles that are unobservant of the respect and reverence due to sacred subjects, nor hopeless, doubt-creating, and pessimistic accounts that create deviations in the heart.

CHILDREN, HAVE YOU EVER THOUGHT? .4.

# LET'S LEARN OUR ISLAM

## HARUN YAHYA

*January 2004*

# CONTENTS

# INTRODUCTION

D ear Children, in this book we will be discussing important issues which you must think hard about...

At school, your teachers first teach you the alphabet. Then come numbers and mathematics lessons. But have you ever wondered why you go to school and learn all these?

Most of you will say that these things are essential in order to have a decent profession when you grow up. That means you are almost sure that you will grow up someday. Indeed, the day may come when children around you will start calling you, "Aunt, grandfather or uncle..." in the same way you address your aunt, grandfather, or uncle, right now. In other words, you will one day grow up if Allah has destined you to do so.

However, you won't continue growing old for ever.

Everyone grows old gradually, but when the day comes they leave this world and start a new life in the hereafter. This also holds true for you. After these days of childhood, you may grow into a young man or woman and then even reach the age of your grandparents. Then will come the time when you will start living your life in the hereafter.

You go to school to prepare for the future. It is important for every individual to make these preparations. However, all these efforts are limited to the life of this world only. What about the things you need for your next life? You must prepare for the hereafter as well. Have you ever thought about that?

When you grow up, you will need to earn your living, which means you must have a profession. This is why you go to school. Likewise, to have a happy life in the hereafter, there are certain things you must do. The foremost of these is immediately to start coming to know Allah, the Exalted, and how our Lord wants us to conduct ourselves.

Here, in this book we will talk about the power of Allah Who created your mother, father, friends, all other people, animals, plants, and in short all living things, the earth, the sun, the moon and the entire universe. We will talk about the might and infinite knowledge of our Lord and what He wants us to do and not to do. Do not forget, these are very important matters, which will benefit you greatly!

# ALLAH CREATED ALL OF US

You often hear people referring to "Allah." They usually form sentences such as, "May Allah bless you," "If Allah wills," "Insha'Allah," "May Allah forgive you" and so on.

These are the statements that are used when one remembers Allah, prays to Him or exalts Him.

For example, "May Allah protect you" expresses the fact that Allah has infinite power over you and every being-animate or inanimate-around you. It is Allah Who can save you, your mother, father and your friends from evil. For this reason, this phrase is often used when mentioning a natural disaster or similar unwelcome event. Think for a moment: Could your mother,

12

father or anyone else you know prevent a natural disaster, for example, a flood? They certainly could not, because only Allah makes such events happen to man and, similarly, only He can prevent them.

The word "insha'Allah" means "if Allah wills." Therefore, when we say that we are going to do something or not going to do something, it is essential we say, "Insha'Allah." This is because only Allah knows the future and thus creates it as He wills. Nothing happens except what He wills.

When one of our friends, for instance, says, "I will certainly go to school tomorrow," he or she is making a mistake, because we cannot know what Allah wills him or her to do in the future. Maybe he or she will be sick and unable to go to school, or atrocious weather conditions may suspend classes.

For this reason we say "insha'Allah" when expressing our intentions for the future, and thereby acknowledge that Allah knows everything, that everything happens only by His Will and that we can never know anything beyond what Allah teaches us. This way, we show due respect to our Lord, Who possesses infinite might and knowledge.

In the verses of the Qur'an, Allah informs us that He wants us to say "insha'Allah" (If Allah wills):

**Never say about anything, "I am doing that tomorrow," without adding "If Allah wills." Remember your**

**Lord when you forget, and say, "Hopefully my Lord will guide me to something closer to right guidance than this." (Surat al-Kahf: 23-24)**

You may not know a lot about these issues, but that is not really important. In order for you to come to know Allah, all you need to do is to look around and think.

Everywhere is full of beauty showing us the attributes of Allah and His infinite might. Think about a lovely white rabbit, the smiling faces of dolphins, the glorious colours of butterfly wings or the blue seas, green forests, various kinds of flowers and the other innumerable beauties in the world. It is Allah Who creates all of these. Allah has created the entire universe you see-the world and the creatures in it-from nothing. Therefore, looking at the beauty that He creates, you can see His infinite might.

It is a fact that our own existence is evidence of Allah's existence. So let us first think about our existence and how Allah has created us so perfectly.

# The Existence of Man

Have you ever wondered how man came into existence? You will probably say, "Everyone has a mother and father." But that answer is inadequate. After all, it does not explain how the first mother and father, that is, the first man, came into being. You will most probably have heard some stories on this subject at school or from people around you. Yet the only accurate answer is that it is Allah Who created you. We will dwell on this issue in detail in the coming chapters. For now, there is one thing we must all know; The first human being who appeared on earth was the Prophet Adam, peace be upon him. All human beings are descended from him.

Adam, peace be upon him, was, just like us, a man who walked, talked, prayed and worshipped Allah. Allah first created him and then his wife. Then their children spread all over the world.

Never forget that Allah only needs to give a command in order to create. When He wishes something to be, He gives the command "Be!" and it comes into being. He has enough power to do anything. For example, He created Adam from clay. This is easy for Allah.

However, never forget that there are also people who deny Allah's existence. These people give other answers to the question of how people came into existence. They do not search for the truth.

Does not man recall that
We created him before he
was not anything?
(Surah Maryam: 67)

**If the boy in this cartoon says, "My picture here has been drawn by ink being spilt on a white sheet of paper by pure chance," this will just sound strange, since we know that it is an artist who drew this picture. Similarly, a man sounds strange if he fails to accept that Allah created him.**

If a cartoon character said, "I came into existence when ink was spilt on the paper by chance. The paints were also spilt by chance and formed the colours. That is to say, I do not need anyone to draw my picture or shape me. I can come into being myself, by chance," you would surely not take it seriously. You know that the perfect lines, colours and actions in cartoons cannot be formed by randomly spilling paint here and there, since knocking over an ink bottle only makes a mess; It never forms a fine picture made up of regular lines. For something meaningful and with a purpose to come into being, someone has to think about it, design it and draw it.

To understand all this, you do not need to see the artist and the painter. You automatically understand that the cartoonist has given this character its attributes, shapes and colours, and the faculty of speaking, walking or jumping.

After this example, think seriously about the following: Someone who does not accept that Allah created him is also lying, just like that cartoon character.

Now let's assume that such a person talks to us. Let's see how this man tries to explain how he and everyone else came into existence:

"I, my mother, father, their parents and the very first parents who lived from time immemorial all came into existence by

**Everyone knows that a cartoonist drew all the attributes of cartoon characters, their shapes, colours, and their faculties such as walking, running and jumping.**

chance. Coincidences created our bodies, eyes, ears and all organs."

These words of this man, who denies that Allah created him, are very much like the words of the cartoon character. The only difference is that the character is made up of lines and paint on a sheet of paper. The person who utters these words, on the other hand, is a man made up of cells. But does this make any difference? Isn't the man who utters these words a highly complex organism more perfect than the cartoon character? Doesn't he have more organs? In other words, if it is impossible for a cartoon character to come into being by chance, then it is even more unlikely for this man to have come into being by chance. Now, let's ask this man the following question:

"You have a very wonderful body that functions flawlessly. Your hands can hold objects with great delicacy—much better than the most developed machines. You can run on your feet. You have perfect eyesight, sharper than the highest quality cameras. You never hear a hissing sound in your ears; No hi-fi can produce such a clear sound. Many organs of which you are unaware work together to keep you alive. For instance, although you have no control whatsoever over the functioning of your heart, kidneys or liver, they continually operate flawlessly. Today, hundreds of scientists and engineers are working strenuously to design machines similar to these organs. However, their efforts have achieved nothing. That is to say, you are a flawless creature, the like of which cannot be manufactured by man. How do you account for all this?"

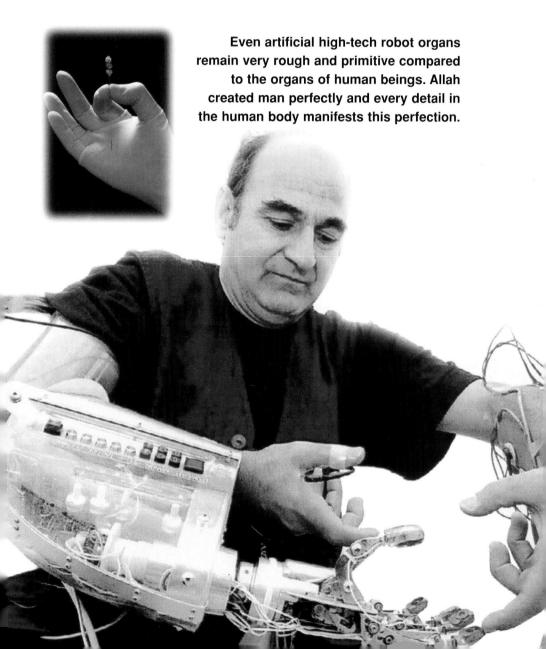

Even artificial high-tech robot organs remain very rough and primitive compared to the organs of human beings. Allah created man perfectly and every detail in the human body manifests this perfection.

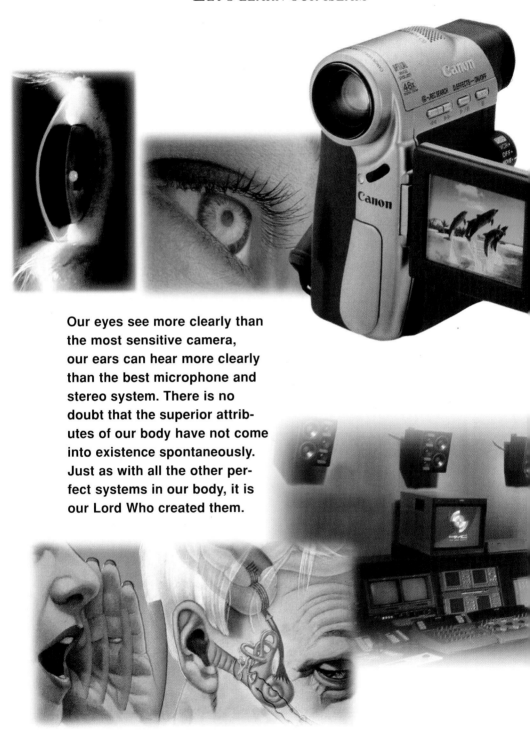

Our eyes see more clearly than the most sensitive camera, our ears can hear more clearly than the best microphone and stereo system. There is no doubt that the superior attributes of our body have not come into existence spontaneously. Just as with all the other perfect systems in our body, it is our Lord Who created them.

The man who denies that Allah creates these things will probably say:

"I also know that we have a flawless body and perfect organs. But I believe in the following: inanimate and unconscious atoms came together by coincidence to form our organs and bodies."

You will doubtless have noticed that these words sound unreasonable and odd. Whatever age he may be or occupation he may have, a person who puts forward such claims obviously fails to think clearly and has mistaken ideas. Surprisingly, one frequently comes across people who believe in such irrational notions.

Since even the simplest machine has a designer, a complex system like man could not have come into existence by chance. There is no doubt that Allah created the first human being. Allah also created the systems within the body of the first man to enable reproduction and the appearance of succeeding generations. Allah ensured the human race would continue by means of a programme inserted in its cells. We also came into existence thanks to this programme created by Allah, and continue to grow up in line with it. What you read about this subject in the following pages will enable you to attain a better understanding of the fact that Allah, Our Creator, possesses infinite power and wisdom.

## The flawless programme in the human body

In the previous page, we mentioned a perfect programme Allah inserted into the human body. Thanks to this programme, every human being has eyes, ears, arms and teeth. Again thanks to this programme, despite some differences in their appearances, all human beings look reasonably similar. We resemble our relatives, and some peoples have their own distinctive characteristics because of this programme. For instance, the Chinese and Japanese generally resemble one another, and Africans have their unique skin colours, facial features, and mouth and eye structures.

Now let's explain what this programme is like with the following example:

**Despite some superficial distinctions between races, everyone shares such basic, unchanging features as the mouth, nose, eyes and ears. Due to the different programmes that Allah put in the human body, everyone enjoys the same fundamental characteristics, although they may look superficially different.**

You must have an idea of the way computers operate. An expert designs the computer. Experts in special factories with the help of advanced technologies also produce complementary components such as the microprocessor, monitor, keyboard, CD, loudspeakers and so on. Now, you have a machine capable of processing highly complex operations. You can either play games or write whatever you want. But for all this to happen, you need software called "programmes." Without these programmes, which are specially prepared by experts, your computer would fail to operate.

**In order for a computer to operate, software called a "programme" is needed. A person lives thanks to the information similar to software that Allah has placed in our genes.**

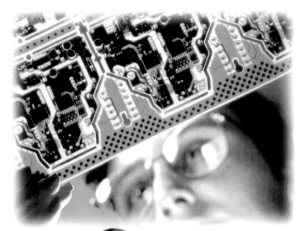

**The human body has a highly complex system far superior to and much more complex than a computer. While nobody claims that this computer came into existence by chance, some people claim that our bodies have acquired these features by chance.**

Furthermore, we know that not every programme is compatible with every type of computer, which means that the programmer must know both the computer and the software compatible with it. As we have seen, one needs both a machine and a proper programme to operate a computer. But more importantly, if nobody designed and produced all these things, your computer would again fail to work.

The human body is similar to a computer. As we said earlier, there is a programme in our cells that brings about our existence. Now the question is, how did it happen that this programme came into existence? The answer is obvious:

26

Allah, the Almighty, specially creates every human being. It is Allah Who has created our bodies as well as the programme that shapes them.

But don't get me wrong. From another point of view, it is quite impossible to compare the human body to a computer. Our bodies are infinitely superior to the most complex computer. Our brain alone, for instance, is many times more complex than a computer.

**The colour of our eyes or our heights as adults are all known even in our mothers' wombs. Our bones, muscles, head, eyes and ears begin to come into existence in just the right place in just the right order. None of our organs makes a mistake and occupies the space of another organ.**

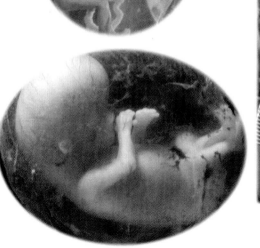

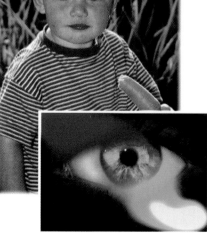

Now let's see how a baby is born into this world:

Initially, there exists a tiny piece of flesh in your mother's womb. In the course of time, this tiny piece of flesh expands and takes shape.

Your height, the colour of your eyes, your eyebrows, the shape of your hands and hundreds of other features are all prede-termined from the very first moment of your existence. All this information is stored in that initial programme Allah placed in your cells. This programme is so flawless and detailed that scientists have only recently come close to understanding how it operates.

In accordance with the programme Allah placed in our bodies, we grow gradually. That is why the growth of our body does not seem odd to us. It takes us years to grow. We would no doubt be astonished if this programme worked faster. The sight of a newborn baby suddenly turning into an old man before our very eyes would be quite amazing.

In compliance with the programme Allah has placed in our bodies, we grow gradually. The sight of a newborn baby suddenly turning into an old person before our very eyes would certainly astonish us.

# How Did Other Living Things Come Into Existence?

Human beings are not by any means the only creatures who exist on earth. There are thousands of other living things, some of which you know and many others you do not. Some of them are all around you; you see them everywhere. Some of them, however, are so far away that you only have the chance to see them in books or movies. But a closer look at these beings would show you that they all have one feature in common. Can you guess what that feature is? We can call it "compatibility." Now, let's enumerate what a living thing is compatible with. They are compatible with:

- The environment in which they live,
- Other living things with which they co-exist,
- The elements that maintain the balance of nature,
- The factors that provide benefits for human beings.

Before expanding on these, let us take a simple example to clarify the meaning of "compatibility." Think about the sockets and plugs in your home. They are perfectly compatible with one another. But how can you tell that they are perfectly compatible with one another? Because there are openings in the socket into which the prongs of the plug fit. Do you think these are enough? The width of the plug's metal prongs is just the same as the width of the openings in the socket. If this were not the case, the plug would never fit the socket. The distance between the plug's prongs and the distance between the socket's openings are also the same. If they were not the same, the plug would never fit in the socket. However, these features alone would not be enough to establish the compatibility of the plug and the socket. If the plug were very long, this would again be a failure in terms of compatibility. If the prongs of the plug were non-metallic, they would fail to conduct the electricity in the socket. If the plug were not made of plastic, then every time you held it you would receive an electric shock. As you see, a lack of compatibility in even the simplest device renders that device inoperative. This means that the same person designed the plug and the socket. And he designed them to be compatible with one another. He made them functional. It is unlikely that the metal and plastic could have come together by coincidence and that they were planned separately and independently of each other, because in that case you could never find a socket and plug compatible with one another.

The compatibility of living things is far more complicated than the compatibility in a socket and plug, because living things contain thousands of systems and organs that have to co-exist harmoniously and work together flawlessly. Any attempt to write down these systems one by one would fill a library of hun-

**Allah created every living being in an environment in which it can survive. Fish can breathe in water, birds can fly in the sky and mammals can live on land.**

dreds of books. Therefore, in the following pages we will dwell in brief on these flawless features of the living things created by Allah:

31

## - Living things are compatible with the environment in which they live

Every living thing, whether on land or in the air, is perfectly compatible with its habitat. This is how they are created. Various perfect systems secure the nutrition, protection and reproduction of living things. That is to say, each living thing is specially designed in accordance with its habitat.

The organs and the lifestyles of living things are all compatible with the conditions in their environment. For instance, birds have perfect wings to fly in the sky. Fish have specially created gills with which to breathe under water. If they had lungs like us, they would drown.

## - Living things are compatible with other living things with which they co-exist

Some birds and insects contribute to the reproduction of plants. That means that, although they are unaware of it, they help the growth of plants. For instance, while visiting one flower after another, bees carry pollen. Thanks to this process, plants are able to reproduce. In some cases, animals perform actions that are beneficial to other animals. Cleaning fish, for instance, clean micro-organisms off the skins of big fish and thus provide the basis for a healthy life for them. This is another form of compatibility.

Bees carry the pollen of the flowers they visit to other flowers. This is the process that ensures the reproduction of flowers. Similarly, cleaning fish clean larger fish.

There is a balance in the creation of living things in nature. Owing to this flawless balance, they can survive as species for millions of years.

**- Living things are compatible with the elements that secure the balance of nature**

No living thing, apart from man, disturbs the balance in nature. Furthermore, they are created with features that maintain that balance. Yet, the balance of the earth is always vulnerable to man's ignorant behaviour. For instance, if man hunts a species beyond reasonable limits, that species becomes extinct. The extinction of that species causes its prey to increase in numbers far too much, which in time endangers the lives of human beings and even nature itself. So, there is an innate balance in the creation of living things; They are totally compatible with the balance of nature, but man alone has the potential to destroy that delicate balance.

**- Living things are compatible with the factors that provide benefits for human beings.**

For instance, think about how good honey is for you. How do bees know that you need such a type of nutrition, and how do

**We need nutrients such as meat, milk, eggs, chicken, honey, vegetables and fruit every day. Many other fundamental sources of nutrition are blessings Allah created for us, in return for which we need to give thanks to Him.**

they produce it? Could a chicken, cow or sheep know the nutritional needs of human beings and produce perfect nutrients to meet those needs? Of course not.

This astonishing harmony between living things is obvious evidence that a single Creator creates them. It is thanks to the flawless creation of Allah that these balances exist on earth.

## The Creation of the Universe

We have so far explained Allah's creation of living things. Now, it is time to examine the universe at large. Allah also created the universe in which you, the earth, the sun, the solar system, planets, stars, galaxies and everything else exists.

However, as well as those who oppose the fact of the creation of living things, there are also some people who deny the fact that the universe was created. These people assert that the universe came into existence spontaneously. Moreover, they suggest that it has always existed. Yet, they never offer an explanation for this irrational claim. Their claim is similar to the following example: Imagine that you set sail one day and reached the shores of an island. What would you think if you came across a highly developed city with skyscrapers, surrounded by beautiful parks and greenery? Furthermore, this city was full of theatres, restaurants and railroad lines. You would certainly think that this city had been planned and constructed by intelligent people, would you not? What would you think about someone who says, "Nobody built this city. It has always existed, and at some time in the past we came and inhabited it. Here, we have all our necessities, and they all come into existence spontaneously"?

**Everyone agrees that the modern and highly developed city in the picture could not have come into existence by accident and that it was designed and constructed by expert architects, engineers and builders. No one would claim otherwise.**

You would doubtless think him insane, or else you would think that he has no idea what he is talking about. But never forget that the universe in which we live is incomparably larger than that city. The universe contains an almost uncountable number of planets, stars, comets and satellites of various sorts. That being the case, the claims of a person who says that this flawless universe was not created but has always existed must not remain unanswered. Do you not agree?

37

The universe in which we live is incomparably bigger than the city we saw on the previous page. It also has more glorious structures than this city.

He is the Originator of the
heavens and the earth...
(Surat al-An'am: 101)

In this case, could we say that a flawless universe was not created and that it came into existence spontaneously? Such a claim
would doubtless sound very odd. It is our Lord Who created the
flawless order in the design of the universe.

After reading the section below, you yourself will be able to provide the best answer. Now, let's expand on the subject of the universe and save the answer to the end.

### - Everything Started to Form In a Big Explosion

During the times when people did not have telescopes to make observations of the heavens, they had very little, and very unreliable, information about the remote universe, and they had very different ideas about it. With advances in technology, they attained accurate information about outer space. In the mid-twentieth century, they discovered something very important. The universe has a date of birth, which means that the universe has not always existed. The universe—in other words, the stars, planets and galaxies—started to form at a specific date. Scientists calculated the age of the universe to be 15 billion years.

They named the moment the universe was born the "Big Bang," because 15 billion years ago, when nothing existed, everything suddenly emerged with an explosion from a single point. In brief, matter and the universe, which people assumed to have always existed, had a beginning. At this point, the question arises, "How did they come to understand that it had a beginning?" That was quite easy; The matter that scattered and sped away from other particles of matter with the big explosion is still moving away. Think for a moment! The universe is continuing to expand even at this moment. Imagine the universe as a balloon. If we draw two small spots on this balloon, what happens when you blow it up? The spots on the balloon move away from one another as the balloon expands and its volume increases. As in the case of the balloon, the volume of the universe is also increasing, and everything within it is racing away from everything else. In other words, the distance between the stars, galaxies, stars and meteors is continually increasing.

Imagine that you are watching the expansion of the universe in a cartoon film. How would the universe look if we rewound the film back to the beginning? It would reduce down

**Just as the small spots drawn on a balloon move away from one another as the balloon expands, so celestial bodies move away from one another with the effect of the Big Bang.**

to a single point, would it not? That is exactly what scientists did. They returned to the beginning of the Big Bang and realised that the ever-expanding universe had initially been a single point.

This explosion, called the Big Bang, became the initial point of the existence Allah had predetermined for the "universe." With this explosion, Allah created the particles that made up the universe, and thus matter emerged. It scattered around at tremendous speed. During the initial moments of the explosion, this environment was almost like a soup of matter made up of different particles. But in time this great chaos started to transform into an ordered structure. Allah created atoms from the particles, and eventually stars from the atoms. Allah created the entire universe and everything in it.

**If you think of the expansion of the universe as a film, if you rewound the images back to the beginning you would see that initially there was a single point.**

Let's give an example to clarify all this:

Think of a huge space. It is utterly unlimited. There is only a bowl full of paint in it. Nothing else exists. In the bowl, all sorts of paints are mixed up, forming unusual colours. Imagine that a bomb explodes in this bowl, under the effect of which the paints scatter everywhere in the form of tiny specks. Imagine that millions of paint specks move in all directions in this space. Meanwhile, during this voyage of the small specks, unusual things start to happen. Instead of forming a chaotic mess and ultimately disappearing, they start interacting as if they were intelligent beings. The droplets that initially formed a coloured mixture start to sort themselves into their individual colours. Blues, yellows, reds, and all droplets of the same colour groups collect together and continue to move away. Yet even more unusual things continue to happen: Five hundred blue droplets join together and, in the form of a bigger drop, continue their journey. Meanwhile, three hundred red droplets in one corner and two hundred yellow droplets in another merge and keep scattering around together. These separate groups of colours move away from one another and form beautiful images, as if acting upon someone's orders.

Some droplets come together and form images of stars, others become the picture of a sun, and some others form the planets around this sun. Another group of drops form the image of the Earth, while another forms the moon. If you ever saw such

**The paints in a bowl scatter around as the result of an explosion. Could the paint droplets randomly scattered around spontaneously come together and form the picture we see in outer space? The spontaneous formation of this picture is definitely impossible. Advocating the theory that the universe came into existence by accident is more irrational than suggesting the spontaneous formation of the picture.**

a picture, would you think that an explosion in a bowl of paint had accidentally formed this picture? Nobody would think that possible.

As the story of the paint drops shows, matter came together and formed the perfect picture we see when we look up in the sky, in other words, stars, the sun and planets. But could all these things have happened by themselves?

How could the stars in the sky, the planets, the sun, moon, and earth ever have come into existence as a result of atoms falling together by chance after an explosion? How about your mother, father, friends or birds, cats, bananas or strawberries…? Of course, this is most unlikely to have happened. Such an idea is as nonsensical as claiming that a house was not built by workers, but came into being by the free will of tiles and bricks, and by pure chance. We all know that bricks scattered around by a bomb explosion do not form little huts. They are reduced into stone and soil and, in time, mix back into the earth.

But one point deserves particular attention. As you know, paint drops are unconscious and inanimate matter. It is impossible that drops of paint could spontaneously come together and form pictures. Here, however, we are talking about the formation of conscious and living things. It is certainly highly improbable that living things such as human beings, plants and animals could have come into existence from inanimate matter purely through random chance.

To understand this better, we should consider our own bodies: They are composed of tiny molecules invisible to the eye, such as proteins, fats and water...These make up the cells, and the cells

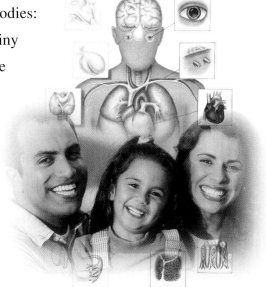

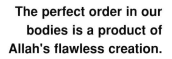

**The perfect order in our bodies is a product of Allah's flawless creation.**

make up our bodies. The perfect order in our bodies is a product of a special design. Allah created our eyes that see, our hands that hold this book and our legs that enable us to walk. Allah predetermined how we would develop in our mothers' wombs, how tall we would be and the colours of our eyes.

## It Is Allah Who Created Everything

If you recall, at the beginning of the book we sought the correct answer to give to a disbelieving person. Now you have the answer. Explosions do not form an orderly picture, but only disrupt an existing one. The order that emerged after the explosion of the universe is even more perfect than the examples

we mentioned—a big city or the bowl of paint. All these cannot be the product of coincidence.

This perfect system could have only been brought into being by the will of Almighty Allah. Allah is able to create anything. He just says to it, "Be!" and it is.

Allah created a beautiful world in a flawless universe for us, and He created animals and plants in it. He created the sun to emit energy and to make us warm. So finely adjusted is the distance of the sun from the earth that were it a little closer our world would be very hot, but if it were any farther away, then we would all freeze.

As scientists uncover more of these facts, we come to know the might of Allah better. That is because matter can neither make decisions nor carry them out. This means there is a Creator Who designs and creates this universe. Matter, the underlying substance of the stars, human beings, animals, plants and of everything, whether animate or inanimate, is all under Allah's control. That is why everything on earth is orderly. Because everything is created by Allah, the Maker and the Giver of Form.

## Allah Created Everyone With A Destiny

At the beginning of the book, we referred to how Allah created Adam, peace be upon him. All human beings are descended from him. Allah has granted people life in this world to test them, and sent them messengers to communicate their responsibilities.

**Everyone is put to the test in this world by the events he experiences. In other words, we are put to the test in our reactions to the incidents we encounter, the way we speak and our steadfastness in the face of difficulties: In brief, whether we conduct ourselves correctly.**

This test will serve to determine our lot in the afterlife.

But the test in this world has a very important secret. As a great mercy and comfort granted to mankind, Allah created destiny.

**Everything a person experiences from his birth to his death is determined by destiny. You can think of this like a film strip. If we take a film strip and look at it from a distance, we can see the beginning, middle and end of events at the same time.**

49

Destiny, that is, all the incidents one experiences throughout life, is predetermined by Allah even before one's birth. For each person, Allah creates his or her unique destiny.

To better understand this, we can liken it to a movie recorded on a videotape cassette. Both the beginning and the end of this movie are already known, but we can only know them after watching the film. This also holds true for destiny. Everything a person will do throughout his life, all the incidents he encounters, the schools he will attend, the houses in which he will live, and the moment of his death are all predetermined.

All incidents that happen to a person, whether good or evil, are predetermined in Allah's knowledge. Each person is put to the test in compliance with this scenario specifically written for him. To sum up, in accordance with this scenario, man goes through a series of incidents, and his faith, and then his actions as well as his reactions to these incidents, determine his lot in the afterlife.

Knowledge of destiny is a great source of comfort for man. It is a blessing from Allah. For this reason, there is no need for man to feel sorry for incidents whose outcomes are already preordained or to worry over events that do not go well. To those who show patience in the face of ordeals, aware that nothing happens without Allah's will, Allah gives the glad tidings of the Garden (Paradise). The messengers of Allah set the best examples in this respect. Allah gives such people the glad tidings of the Garden due to their exemplary faith and correct behaviour.

# ALLAH SENT MESSENGERS AND BOOKS

I n previous chapters, we provided examples and evidence that help us to ponder and grasp something of Allah's might and grandeur. The reason why Allah endowed us with the faculties of thinking and reasoning is in order for us to come to know Him. Allah has also sent us the revealed Books through which He introduces Himself. He communicates what He expects from us in these Books. Allah commissioned and sent messengers who set examples for their peoples with their excellent conduct. Through these messengers, the pure message and revelation of Allah provide guidance for mankind.

It is difficult to know exactly how many messengers Allah sent, although there are traditions relating that, for example, there have been three hundred and thirteen messengers and a much greater number of prophets throughout history. We only know the names of the prophets mentioned in the Qur'an, the last revelation sent by Allah. Allah provides us with knowledge of the lives of the prophets to allow us to understand their conduct. Through the messengers He sent, Our Lord conveys to us the right way of living and how to conduct ourselves correctly in this world. Only through Allah's communications can we know how to conduct ourselves, and which types of behaviour are better and more in compliance with the values of the Qur'an. It is only through His communications that we can ever know the behaviour that earn Allah's good pleasure and His infinite reward as well as those that lead to punishment.

In the Qur'an, Allah informs us that throughout history He sent His messengers to all communities, and that they warned them. These messengers summoned their people to worship

The only book revealed by Allah to have survived completely intact is the Qur'an.

Allah, to pray to Him and to comply with His commands. He also made clear to them that otherwise they would be punished. In brief, they warned the disbelievers and those who engaged in wicked deeds, and they gave glad tidings to believers that they would be rewarded. *(The Garden and the Fire will be dealt with extensively in the following sections.)* The last prophet Allah sent to mankind was the Prophet Muhammad, may Allah bless him and grant him peace. The Qur'an is the last revealed Book.

The earlier revelations from Allah have lost their authenticity, since ignorant people and those with bad intentions have incorporated their own words and extra pieces into them. Therefore, their originals, the true revelations that were initially sent to the peoples, did not survive to our day. But Allah sent us the Qur'an, the Book that is impossible to alter.

The Prophet Muhammad, may Allah bless him and grant him peace, and later Muslims preserved the Qur'an very well. The Qur'an is so clear that everyone can understand it. When we read the Qur'an, we can immediately understand that it is the Speech of Allah. The Qur'an, which has survived completely intact, is under Allah's protection and it is the only revealed

Book for which people will be responsible until the Day of Judgment.

Today all Muslims, wherever they are, read the very same Qur'an; Not a single discrepancy can be found in one word or letter. The Qur'an revealed to the Messenger, may Allah bless him and grant him peace, and compiled by the Caliph Abu Bakr and then later written out by the Caliph Uthman, may Allah be pleased with them, who lived 1,400 years ago, and the Qur'an we read today are identical. There is a one-to-one correspondence between them. This means, from the day the Qur'an was revealed to the Prophet Muhammad, peace be upon him, it has survived intact. That is because Allah protected the Qur'an from evil people who intended to alter it or incorporate extra bits in it. In one verse, Allah informs us that He preserves the Qur'an specially:

**It is We Who have sent down the Reminder [i.e., the Qur'an] and We Who will preserve it. (Surat Al-Hijr: 9)**

With the word "We" in this verse, Allah refers to Himself. There is no other god besides Allah, He has no partner. He is the Almighty Allah, the Originator of everything and the One Who encompasses everything in His knowledge.

In some parts of the Qur'an, Allah refers to Himself with the word "I," and in some others with the word, "We." In Arabic, which is the language of the Qur'an, the word "We" is also employed to refer to a single person with the purpose of arousing feelings of might and respect in the listener. There is a similar case in English known as "The Royal We." In the succeeding sections of this book, we will give you examples of verses (of the Qur'an) and surahs (chapters of the Qur'an). They are the most correct words because they are the words of Allah, the One Who knows us better than we do ourselves.

In the Qur'an, Allah wants us to take lessons from the lives of the prophets. One verse reads:

**There is instruction in their [i.e., messengers'] stories for people of intelligence... (Surah Yusuf: 111)**

The type of person to whom Allah draws our attention in this verse is a person who knows that the Qur'an is the Speech of Allah and thereby thinks, exercises his reason and strives to learn the Qur'an and live by its commands.

Allah holds the people to whom He sends His messengers responsible for complying with His commands. Having received Allah's revelations, people will have no right to put forward excuses on the Day of Judgment. That is because the messengers of Allah convey to their peoples the knowledge of the existence of Allah and of what He expects from people. Once a person hears this message, he is responsible for it. This is related in the Qur'an as follows:

Have they not seen how many generations We destroyed before them...? (Surat al-An'am: 6)

**Messengers bringing good news and giving warning, so that people will have no argument against Allah after the coming of the Messengers. Allah is Almighty, All-Wise. (Surat an-Nisa: 165)**

Allah created many groups of people on earth. Some of these groups refused what their messengers brought to them and denied that they were messengers at all. Because they did not listen to their words and comply with Allah's commands, they were punished. Through His messengers, Allah also warned these rebellious people of a terrible life in this world. Despite this, they continued to oppose their messengers and slander them. Furthermore, they became so violent as in some cases even to murder them. Upon this, Allah gave them the punishment they deserved, and, in time, new communities replaced them. In the Qur'an, the situation of such communities is related as follows:

**Have they not seen how many generations We destroyed before them which We had established on the earth far more firmly than We have established you? We sent down heaven upon them in abundant rain and made rivers flow under them. But We destroyed them for their wrong actions and raised up further generations after them. (Surat al-An'am: 6)**

In coming chapters, we will dwell on the exemplary behaviour of the prophets who struggled against these rebellious communities.

# The First Human Being and
# The First Prophet: Adam

As you will remember, while we were talking about the creation of man, we said that the first man on earth was Adam, peace be upon him. Adam was also the first prophet. That is, Allah also sent a messenger to the very first community He created on earth and taught them their deen (religion) and how to become slaves devoted to Allah.

Allah taught Adam how to speak and all the names. This is related in the Qur'an as follows:

**He taught Adam the names of all things... (Surat al-Baqara: 31)**

This is surely very important. Among all living things, only man has the faculty of speech. Speaking is a feature peculiar to human beings. Thanks to the fact that Allah initially gave this faculty to Adam, it became possible for man to know the objects around him and to give names to them.

The generations succeeding Adam could also speak, had feelings, felt sorry or excited, wear clothes, used tools and devices and had talent for music and the arts. Musical instruments such as the flute, wall drawings and some other objects that scientists have found with the remains of ancient human beings prove that they were people like us. In other words, contrary to the claims of some people, the first human beings had never been wild creatures, half-ape/half-man.

You know that neither an ape nor any other being can speak, think or act like a human being. Allah gave all these faculties especially to man. (For further information on this subject you can refer to the book, *Wonders of Allah's Creation by Harun Yahya*).

**In this book, you can read about the falsity of the theory of evolution, which asserts that living beings came into existence by accident.**

But some people who are not willing to accept the fact that the first human being was Adam put forward some claims of their own: They fabricated a false identity for the first human being. According to their imaginary scenarios, human beings and apes sprang from the same living thing, that is, they had a common ancestor, and evolved in time into their current states. If you ask how this unusual happening occurred, they give a single answer: "It happened by chance." When you ask if there is any evidence to prove this claim, they provide none. To conclude, there is not a single remain proving that man evolved from another being.

**There is no difference between ants or fish living in our day and their fossilised relatives shown in the pictures.**

If you ask, "What are these remains from the past?," there is a ready answer: Some living things leave traces behind when they die, and these traces, which we call fossils, remain for millions of years without changing. However, for this to happen, that living thing must suddenly be entrapped in an oxygen-free environment. For instance, if a bird on the ground had been abruptly covered by a heap of sand millions of years ago, the remains of that bird could have survived to our day. Similarly, there are substances secreted from trees called resins. Sometimes, this honey-like substance covers an insect and turns into the hard material called amber, which preserves the dead insect for millions of years. This is the way we gather information about living beings of ancient times. These remains are called "fossils."

Those who suggest that the first human being came into existence from an ape-like creature can never provide any fossils proving this claim. In other words, no one has ever found a fossil belonging to an unusual creature that was half-ape/half-human. But these people have produced false fossils, pictures and drawings to cover up this falsehood, and have even put them into school textbooks.

All these frauds were gradually uncovered one by one and made public as scientific frauds. Because such people are

unwise and obstinate, it is almost impossible for them to accept Allah's existence and to realise that He creates everything. Although the number of such people is diminishing steadily, there are still some who strive to disseminate their flawed views through periodicals, books and newspapers, and also in schools. To make people believe in their flawed views, they insist on their arguments and assert that they have scientific validity. However, each piece of research done and evidence provided by intelligent scientists prove that the ape did not evolve into man.

Adam, the first man, whom Allah specially created, was in all ways the same as contemporary man; He was in no way different. These are the facts Allah communicates to us in the Qur'an. There is yet another very important issue Allah informs us about Adam: The story of Adam and Satan, the enemy of mankind.

## Man's Greatest Enemy: Satan

You may already know about Satan, but do you know that he also knows you very well and resorts to every method to tempt you? Do you know that the actual purpose of Satan, who pretends to be your friend, is to deceive you? Let's start from the very beginning and remind ourselves why Satan is our enemy. For this purpose, we will turn to the story about Adam and Satan in the Qur'an.

In the Qur'an, Satan is the general name given until the Day of Judgment to all beings who have committed themselves to lead man astray. Iblis is the principal evil being who rebelled against Allah when He created Adam.

According to the Qur'anic account, Allah created Adam and then called the angels to prostrate to him. The angels complied with Allah's command, but Iblis refused to prostrate to Adam. He impiously asserted that he was superior to man. Because of his disobedience and insolence, he was banished from Allah's sight.

Before leaving Allah's presence, Iblis requested time from Allah to lead people astray. The purpose of Iblis is to tempt people and thus to make them turn away from the right path within the period of time granted to him. He will try anything to make the majority of people subject to himself. Allah proclaims that He will send Satan and his followers to the Fire. These things are related in the Qur'an as follows:

**We created you and then formed you and then We said to the angels, "Prostrate before Adam," and they prostrated—except for Iblis. He was not among those who prostrated.**

**He [Allah] said, "What prevented you from prostrating when I commanded you to?" He [Iblis] replied, "I am**

better than him. You created me from fire and You created him from clay."

He [Allah] said, "Descend from Heaven. It is not for you to be arrogant in it. So get out! You are one of the abased." He said, "Grant me a reprieve until the day they are raised up." He [Allah] said, "You are one of the reprieved."

He said, "By Your misguidance of me, I will lie in ambush for them on Your straight path. Then I will come at them, from in front of them and behind them, from their right and from their left. You will not find most of them thankful."

He [Allah] said, "Get out of it, reviled and driven out. As for those of them who follow you, I will fill up the Fire with every one of you." (Surat al-A'raf: 11-18)

After being banished from Allah's sight, Satan set upon the struggle that would last until the Day of Judgment. Since then, he has cunningly approached people, schemed to lead them astray and used unprecedented methods for this end. As you now understand better, Satan is a foe that can approach man very cunningly. For this reason, you have to be watchful to escape him.

Never forget that Satan is lying in ambush right now to

scheme against you. He tries to stop you reading this book and thinking over what you read. He is trying to hinder you from doing good deeds, and to get you to become disrespectful and disobedient to your elders, and to hinder you from giving thanks to Allah, praying and always telling the truth. Never allow Satan to deceive you and to hinder you from becoming a person of good character and listening to the voice of your conscience.

You must take refuge in Allah and ask help from Him when an evil thought occurs to you or when you find yourself unwilling to do a good deed, since all these are the cunning tricks of Satan. Never forget that Satan can exercise no authority over those who have faith.

## The Prophet Nuh (Noah)

Nuh, peace be upon him, like all the other prophets, summoned his people to the true path. He told them that they must have faith in Allah, that He is the Creator of everything, that they must worship none but Him, otherwise they would be punished. This is related in the Qur'an as follows:

**We sent Nuh to his people: "I am a clear warner to you. Worship none but Allah. I fear for you the punishment of a painful day." (Surah Hud: 25-26)**

Despite all his warnings, only a few people believed in Nuh. Upon this, Allah commanded Nuh to build a great ship.

66

Allah informed him that the people of faith would be saved in that ship.

Nuh's building a ship despite there being no sea in that area surprised those people who had no faith in Allah, and they therefore ridiculed him. Those who had no faith did not know what would happen to them, but Allah did. When the ship was built, heavy rain poured for days and water rose over the land, flooding everything. This historical disaster has been confirmed by scientists. In the Middle East, much evidence has been uncovered revealing that many of today's mountains were once covered with water.

On television, you have probably seen many floods in different corners of the world. In the face of such a disaster, people generally get up on roofs and wait for help. In such a situation only helicopters or boats can rescue them. In the time of the Prophet Nuh, peace be upon him, however, it was only the Ark that could have saved them. This disaster, which is called "Nuh's flood," was actually a punishment specially created by Allah to punish people who did not believe in Nuh. Because they expected help from other than Allah, none of the insolent people who turned a deaf ear to Allah's warnings embarked on Nuh's Ark. They did not put their trust in Allah, but relied on other beings.

Unless Allah wills it, nothing can protect us. The people at that time who denied this, climbed mountains or moved to higher regions, but still could not save themselves from drowning.

A very few people believed in Allah and put their trust in Him, which led them to embark on the ship with Nuh and save themselves. Complying with Allah's command, they took a pair from each animal species with them. This is related in the Qur'an as follows:

> Before them the people of Nuh denied the truth. They denied Our slave [i.e., Nuh], saying, "He is a madman," and he was driven away with jeers.

> He called upon his Lord: "I am overwhelmed, so help me!"

> So We opened the gates of heaven with torrential water and made the earth burst forth with gushing springs.

And the waters met together in a way which was decreed.

We bore him on a planked and well-caulked ship, which ran before Our eyes—a reward for him who had been rejected.

We left it as a Sign. But is there any rememberer there?

How terrible were My punishment and warnings! (Surat al-Qamar: 9-16)

All the prophets who were sent to their individual communities communicated basically the same teaching and summoned their people to worship Allah and to obey the prophets. In return

for their services, they asked for no wages since those people sent by Allah to communicate His Words do not do so. They render their services only because they love Allah and fear Him. Meanwhile, they face many difficulties: Their people slander them and subject them to cruel treatment. Furthermore, some

70

peoples plotted to kill the prophets sent to them, and some even dared to do so. Yet because the prophets feared only Allah and no one else, no hardship daunted them. They never forgot that Allah would reward them bountifully both in this world and beyond.

# The Prophet Ibrahim (Abraham)

In this section, we will dwell on various attributes of some prophets to whom Allah draws our attention in the Qur'an.

Ibrahim, peace be upon him, was one of these prophets. When he was young and there was no one around him to remind him of Allah's existence, he examined the heavens and that led him to recognise that Allah creates everything. This is related in the Qur'an as follows:

**When night covered him he saw a star and said, "This is my Lord!" Then when it set he said, "I do not love what sets."**

**Then when he saw the moon come up he said, "This is my Lord!" Then when it set he said, "If my Lord does not guide me, I will be one of the misguided people."**

**Then when he saw the sun come up he said, "This is my Lord! This is greater!" Then when it set he said, "My people, I am free of what you associate with Allah! I have turned my face to Him Who brought the heavens and earth into being, a pure natural believer. I am not of those who associate others with Allah." (Surat al-An'am: 76-79)**

Ibrahim, peace be upon him, told his people not to worship any other god than Allah:

**Recite to them the story of Ibrahim when he said to his father and his people,**

**"What do you worship?"**

**They said, "We worship idols and will continue to cling to them."**

**He said, "Do they hear you when you call or do they help you or do you harm?"**

**They said, "No, but this is what we found our fathers doing."**

He [Ibrahim] said, "Have you really thought about what you worship, you and your fathers who came before?

They are all my enemies—except for the Lord of all the worlds:

He who created me and guides me;

**He who gives me food and gives me drink;**

**and when I am ill, it is He who heals me;**

**He who will cause my death, then give me life;**

**He who I sincerely hope will forgive my mistakes on the Day of Reckoning." (Surat ash-Shu'ara: 69-82)**

The enemies of Ibrahim attempted to kill him when he called them to have faith in Allah. They lit a big fire and cast him into it. But Allah protected him and saved him from the fire. This is related in the Qur'an as follows:

**The only answer of his people was to say: "Kill him or burn him!" But Allah rescued him from the fire. There are certainly Signs in that for people who are believers. (Surat al-'Ankabut: 24)**

**We said, "Fire, be coolness and peace for Ibrahim!" (Surat al-Anbiya: 69)**

It is Allah Who creates and controls everything. By Allah's will the fire did not burn Ibrahim. This is a miracle of Allah and a manifestation of His might. Everything on earth occurs by Allah's will. Nothing can happen without His Will and control. If He does not will it, one can neither harm nor kill another person. Allah informs us in the Qur'an:

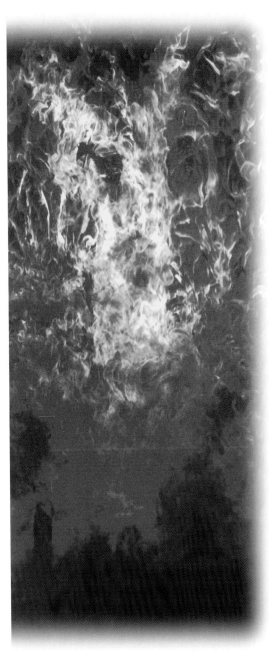

**No self can die except with Allah's permission, at a predetermined time...** **(Surah Al 'Imran: 145)**

He did not die although he was cast into the fire, since his time of death as predetermined by Allah had not yet come. Allah saved him from the fire.

In one verse, Allah relates to us that Ibrahim was a man of exemplary character:

**Ibrahim was forbearing, compassionate, penitent. (Surah Hud: 75)**

Allah loves people who are wholeheartedly devoted to Him. As the verse makes clear, not being rebellious, having a good character, and being submissive to Allah's commandments are favourable attributes in the sight of Allah.

# The Prophet Musa (Moses)

Musa, peace be upon him, is a prophet to whom Allah frequently refers in the Qur'an. Allah revealed to Musa the Torah. But today, the Torah of the Jews and the Old Testament of the Christian Bible have lost their original authenticity, since the words and interpolations of man have been incorporated into them. But Jews and Christians today read these distorted books assuming them to be from the original book revealed by Allah. The Jews have turned from the right path because the book in which they believe is no longer the revealed book brought by the Prophet Musa, peace be upon him.

We know everything about the life and good character of Musa from the Qur'an. As the Qur'an informs us, the kings of ancient Egypt were called "Pharaoh." The majority of the pharaohs were very arrogant people who did not believe in Allah and who considered

**After Musa's death, some people with bad intentions changed the Torah. That is why the Torah and the Old Testament people read today are very different from the original book revealed to Musa, peace be upon him.**

**A king in ancient Egypt was called a "Pharaoh." The majority of the pharaohs were very arrogant people who did not believe in Allah and who considered themselves divine.**

themselves divine. Allah sent Musa to one of the cruellest of these rulers.

One important point we need to dwell on while reading the verses about the life of Musa is "destiny." The following events led him to the palace of Pharaoh:

At the time Musa was born, Pharaoh ordered his soldiers to kill every male baby born in his land. Musa, peace be upon him, was one of those who were in danger. Allah told his mother to leave Musa in a chest in the river and assured her that He would finally return to her as a prophet. His mother placed Musa in a chest and left him in the water. This chest floated randomly on the water and some time later reached the shore at Pharaoh's palace, where Pharaoh's wife found him. She took the baby and decided to bring him up in the palace. Thus, unaware, the Pharaoh undertook to look after the person who would later communicate Allah's revelation to him and oppose his flawed views. Allah encompasses everything with His knowledge, and

**The children of Israel were enslaved by Pharaoh in Egypt. Above you can see these people who were subjected to hard labour.**

He also knew that Pharaoh would find Musa, peace be upon him, and bring him up in his palace.

When Musa was born, Allah knew that he would be left in the river, that Pharaoh would find him and that Musa would ultimately become a prophet. This was how Allah predetermined Musa's destiny and He communicated this to his mother.

At this point, we must pay attention to the fact that every detail in his life happened according to the destiny Allah had predetermined.

When he grew into a young man, Musa left Egypt. After some time, Allah made him a prophet and messenger and sup-

ported him with his brother, Harun, peace be upon them both.

Both of them went to Pharaoh and communicated Allah's message to him. This was really a difficult task since without any hesitation they called on a cruel ruler to believe in Allah and to worship Him. This call of the Messenger Musa, peace be upon him, is related as follows:

**And then, after them, We sent Musa with Our Signs to Pharaoh and his ruling circle but they wrongfully rejected them. See the final fate of the corrupters!**

**Musa said, "Pharaoh! I am truly a Messenger from the Lord of all the worlds, duty bound to say nothing about Allah except the truth. I have come to you with a Clear Sign from your Lord. So send the tribe of Israel away with me." (Surat al-A'raf: 103-105)**

Pharaoh was an arrogant and proud man. Assuming that he held everything under his control, he rebelled against Allah. Allah had granted all his possessions, his strength and his lands to him, but because Pharaoh was unwise, he failed to understand this.

Pharaoh opposed Musa and had no faith in Allah, and he was, as mentioned earlier, a very cruel man. He made the Children of Israel his slaves. When it became clear that Pharaoh was intending to exterminate Musa and all the believers, they

Cruel Pharaoh arrested those who believed in Musa, peace be upon him, and enslaved them.

fled from Egypt under the leadership of Musa. Musa, peace be upon him, and the Children of Israel were caught between the sea and the soldiers of Pharaoh who were pursuing them. But even in such a desperate situation, Musa never despaired or lost his trust in Allah. Allah miraculously divided the sea in two and opened a path in the sea for the Children of Israel to cross. This was one of the great miracles Allah gave to Musa. Once the Children of Israel had reached the other shore, the parted sea returned, drowning Pharaoh and his soldiers.

Allah relates this miraculous event in the Qur'an as follows:

When it became clear that Pharaoh was thinking of exterminating all the believers, they fled from Egypt under the leadership of Musa, peace be upon him.

**Such was the case with Pharaoh's people and those before them. They denied their Lord's Signs so We destroyed them for their wrong actions. We drowned Pharaoh's people. All of them were wrongdoers. (Surat al-Anfal: 54)**

At the moment Pharaoh realised he would die, he stated that he believed in Allah and thus tried to save himself. We do not know whether this regret he felt at the last moment was of any use, since Allah only forgives us when our regret is sincere

Musa and the Children of Israel were caught between the sea and
the soldiers of the Pharaoh pursuing them. But even in such a
desperate situation, Musa never despaired or lost his trust in
Allah. Miraculously Allah divided the sea in two and opened a
path in the sea for the Children of Israel to cross. This was one of
the great miracles Allah gave Musa. Once the Children of Israel
reached the other shore, the parted sea returned, thus drowning
Pharaoh and his soldiers.

and when it is before the moment of death itself. Allah is the All-Merciful. If regret is only felt at the moment of death and, of course, if is not sincere, such repentance will not save a person. This may have been the case with Pharaoh. But only Allah knows. As this story reveals, we must live to please Allah throughout our lives and avoid falling into Pharaoh's error. If we fail in that, feeling sorry at the moment of death may be of no avail.

## The Prophet Yunus (Jonah)

No matter how desperate and difficult a situation, a person must always trust in Allah and ask Him for help. As we mentioned in the previous section, Musa, peace be upon him, never despaired when he was caught between the armies of Pharaoh and the Red Sea, but he put his trust in Allah. Yunus, peace be upon him, also exemplifies such good character.

Although he was commissioned by Allah to warn them, Yunus, peace be upon him, left his people without warning them. Upon this, Allah put him to the test in several ways: first, he was thrown into the sea from the ship on which he sailed. Then a giant fish swallowed him. This made him feel deep regret for his behaviour; he turned in repentance to Allah, took refuge with Him and prayed to Him. This is related in the Qur'an as follows:

**And [mention] the man of he fish [i.e., Yunus], when he left in anger and thought We would not punish him. He called out in the pitch darkness: "There is no god but You! Glory be to You! Truly I have been one of the wrongdoers."**

**We responded to him and rescued him from his grief. That is how We rescue the believers. (Surat al-Anbiya: 87-88)**

In the Qur'an, Allah relates what would have happened to him if he had not trusted in Allah and prayed to Him:

**Had it not been that he was a man who glorified Allah,**

**He would have remained inside its belly until the Day they are raised again.**

**So We cast him up onto the beach and he was sick;**

**And We caused a gourd tree to grow over him.**

**We sent him to a hundred thousand or even more. (Surat as-Saffat: 143-147)**

Allah rescued Yunus from a truly desperate situation. This is an obvious sign that one must never despair of Allah's help. The experiences of Yunus, peace be upon him, are a lesson for all believers: We must never slacken, no matter what hardship

**Yunus was first thrown from a ship into the sea. Then, a giant fish swallowed him. Allah rescued Yunus, peace be upon him, from that desperate situation.**

we face, and we must always pray to Allah and ask for help from Him.

## The Prophet Yusuf (Joseph)

In the Qur'an, we find a detailed account of the experiences of Yusuf, peace be upon him. Here, we will describe them shortly and see the exemplary character of Yusuf.

88

Yusuf was one of the sons of Ya'qub, peace be upon them both. When he was very young, his brothers threw him into a well because they were jealous of him, and they told their father that a wolf had eaten him. Travellers in a caravan found him in the well and sold him at the palace of a nobleman in Egypt. There, he was later slandered and sent to prison, where he remained for years.

**Travellers in a caravan found Yusuf in a well and sold him at the palace of a nobleman in Egypt.**

He was ultimately found innocent and released. Being a very wise and reliable person and because he was completely exonerated, the ruler of Egypt placed the treasuries and store-houses under his authority. Ultimately, Yusuf forgave his brothers who had exposed him to cruelty and brought them and their father and mother to live with him.

Yusuf, peace be upon him, had an exemplary character. Allah put him to the test in various ways, rescued him from a well from which it was impossible to escape, rescued him from an evil situation by sending him to prison and then rescued him from the prison and restored his good name, finally granting him high rank. In every situation, Yusuf, peace be upon him, turned towards Allah and prayed to Him. Despite his innocence he remained in prison for several years, yet he never forgot that this was a trial from Allah. In prison, he always spoke of Allah's might and grandeur to the people around him. His loyalty and trust in Allah under such harsh conditions shows us his excellent character.

## The Prophet Ayyub (Job)

Being steadfast in the face of what happens to one is a very important attribute peculiar to Muslims. Ayyub, peace be upon him, was tried by the loss of his family and his wealth, and a serious harm that caused him great suffering. Ayyub only asked help from Allah and put his trust in Him. Allah answered his prayer and taught him how to overcome this distress. The exemplary character of Ayyub, peace be upon him, and his prayer are related in the Qur'an as follows:

> **Remember Our slave Ayyub when he called on his Lord: "Satan has afflicted me with exhaustion and suffering."**
>
> **[So he was told] "Stamp your foot! Here is a cool bath and water to drink."**
>
> **...We found him steadfast. What an excellent slave! He truly turned to his Lord. (Surah Sad: 41-44)**

No sooner do some of us encounter disease, hardship or trouble, than we immediately despair. Some people even become rebellious towards Allah. However, these attitudes dis-

please Allah. As the example of Ayyub shows, Allah may send various troubles to His slaves, but such afflictions mature the believer and test his devotion to Allah.

In the face of all afflictions we encounter we must pray to Allah and trust Him. We must be patient like Ayyub, peace be upon him, and turn to Allah. Only then, will Allah ease our troubles and reward us both in this world and in the hereafter.

## The Prophet 'Isa (Jesus)

Allah created 'Isa, peace be upon him, in a special way. As in the example of Adam, Allah created him without a father. This is related in the Qur'an as follows:

**The likeness of 'Isa in Allah's sight is the same as Adam. He created him from earth and then He said to him, "Be!" and he was. (Surah Al 'Imran: 59)**

In the Qur'an, 'Isa, peace be upon him, is referred to as the "Son of Maryam." Maryam (Mary) was a noble woman who is shown by Allah to all women as an example. She was a very chaste woman and a devoted believer in Allah. Allah gave her 'Isa through the angel Jibril, miraculously without a father, and the glad tidings that her son would become a prophet.

Allah made 'Isa a prophet and revealed to him the Injil, one of the revealed books Allah sent to mankind. (After the disappearance of 'Isa, the Injil was also altered by people. Today, we do not have the original Injil, and the books the Christians call the Gospels are not really reliable.) Allah ordered 'Isa to summon people to the true path and granted him many miracles. He spoke when he was in the cradle and told people about Allah. 'Isa also gave the glad tidings of Muhammad (Ahmad), may Allah bless him and grant him peace, the Messenger of Allah to succeed him, which is related in the Qur'an as follows:

**And when 'Isa son of Maryam said, "Tribe of Israel, I am the Messenger of Allah to you, confirming the Torah which came before me and giving you the good news of a Messenger after me whose name is Ahmad." When he brought them the Clear Signs, they said, "This is downright magic." (Surat as-Saff: 6)**

In his time, there were very few people who believed in 'Isa or helped him. The enemies of 'Isa devised plots to kill him.

They thought that they had captured and crucified him. But, in the Qur'an, Allah relates to us that they did not kill him:

**...and their saying, "We killed the Messiah, 'Isa son of Maryam, Messenger of Allah." They did not kill him and they did not crucify him but it was made to seem so to them. Those who argue about him are in doubt about it. They have no real knowledge of it, just conjecture. But they certainly did not kill him. (Surat an-Nisa: 157)**

After the disappearance of 'Isa, peace be upon him, his enemies tried to change the revelation he had brought. They started to portray 'Isa and Maryam as supernatural beings, and even as "gods." Still today, there are those who hold these false beliefs. In the words of 'Isa, Allah informs us in the Qur'an that these are wrong beliefs:

94

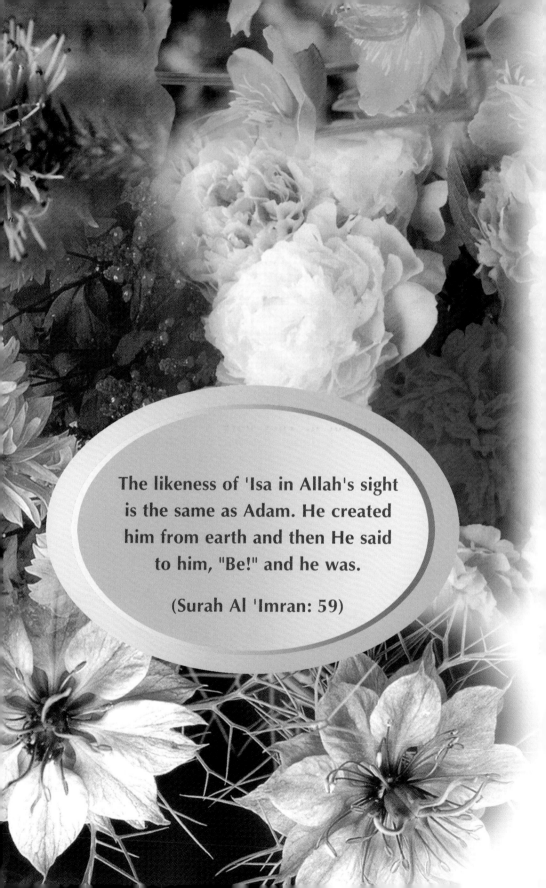

The likeness of 'Isa in Allah's sight is the same as Adam. He created him from earth and then He said to him, "Be!" and he was.

(Surah Al 'Imran: 59)

And when Allah says, " 'Isa son of Maryam! Did you say to people, 'Take me and my mother as gods besides Allah?'" he will say, "Glory be to You! It is not for me to say what I have no right to say! If I had said it, then You would have known it. You know what is in my self but I do not know what is in Your Self. You are the Knower of all unseen things. I said to them nothing but what You ordered me to say: 'Worship Allah, my Lord and your Lord.' I was a witness against them as long as I remained among them, but when You took me back to You, You were the One watching over them. You are Witness of all things." (Surat al-Ma'ida: 116-117)

After his disappearance, the number of people who believed in him increased considerably, but today they are on the wrong path because they follow the Bible, which has been altered through additions and deletions. The only right path remaining today is the path that the Prophet Muhammad, may Allah bless him and grant him peace, summoned us to, which is communicated in the Qur'an, because it is the only unaltered revelation of Allah.

## The Messenger of Allah: Muhammad

We know a lot more about the Messenger of Allah, Muhammad, may Allah bless him and grant him peace, since he is the last prophet and lived only 1,400 years ago. People altered and distorted all the religions Allah revealed before him. That is why the last Book for which people will be held responsible until the Day of Judgment was sent to our Prophet, may Allah bless him and grant him peace: to set right all the errors that had been incorporated in the old religions. Allah communicated what He demands from His slaves through the Qur'an.

Our Prophet, may Allah bless him and grant him peace, also encountered many difficulties while communicating the message of Allah to his people. Many groundless accusations were made against him, despite the fact that he asked for no wages from people and had no worldly interests.

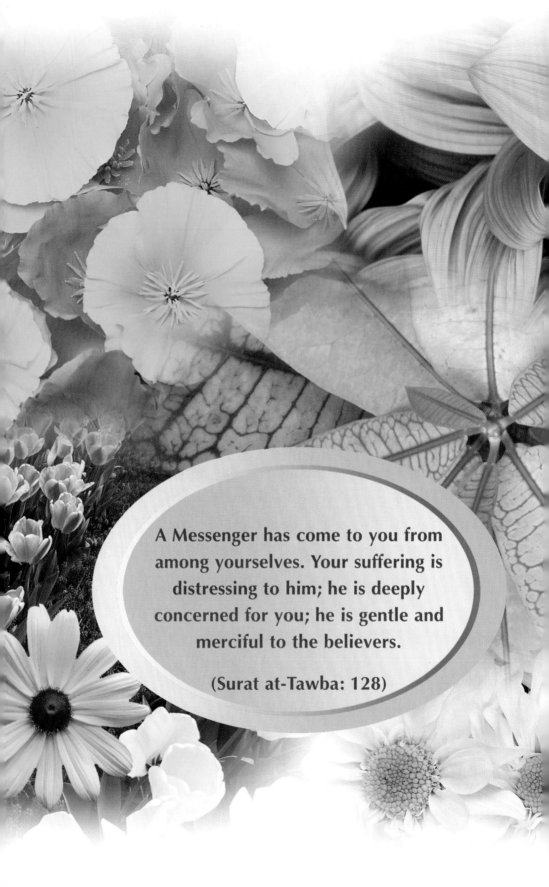

A Messenger has come to you from among yourselves. Your suffering is distressing to him; he is deeply concerned for you; he is gentle and merciful to the believers.

(Surat at-Tawba: 128)

He was forced to migrate from Makkah, the city in which he was born. The first Muslims who followed him were also persecuted, some of them were even tortured and subjected to cruel treatment. But Allah did not allow the disbelievers to do harm to the religion of Islam, which has remained unaltered to this day. In compliance with Allah's promise, every word of the Qur'an has survived completely intact.

The call of the Prophet Muhammad, may Allah bless him and grant him peace, also addresses all people alive today. Allah commanded all people to obey the messengers and, in many verses, stressed that obeying His messengers is actually obeying Him. For this reason, obeying our Prophet, may Allah bless him and grant him peace, -is one of the most important and essential principles of Islam. Heartfelt submission to the commands of our Prophet, may Allah bless him and grant him peace, is surely a manifestation of one's obedience to Allah.

In the Qur'an, Allah introduces us to the superior attributes of our Prophet, which set an example to all people. Some of these verses are as follows:

**A Messenger has come to you from among yourselves. Your suffering is distressing to him; he is deeply concerned for you; he is gentle and merciful to the believers. (Surat at-Tawba: 128)**

**Muhammad is not the father of any of your men, but the Messenger of Allah and the Final Seal of the Prophets. Allah has knowledge of all things. (Surat al-Ahzab: 40)**

**Allah showed great kindness to the believers when He sent a Messenger to them from among themselves to recite His Signs to them and purify them and teach them the Book and Wisdom, even though before that they were clearly misguided. (Surah Al 'Imran: 164)**

With the verses starting with the word, "Say...," Allah commands the Prophet Muhammad, may Allah bless him and grant him peace, how to communicate His message. Through these verses and all the others, our Prophet, may Allah bless him and grant him peace, communicated Allah's message to people. His wife, A'ishah, may Allah be pleased with her said, "His character was the Qur'an." She meant that he completely embodied the Qur'an, and we know that his Sunnah is the practical manifestation of how to obey the Qur'an. In one verse, Allah states that those slaves who fear Allah and want to be forgiven must obey the Messenger of Allah, may Allah bless him and grant him peace:

**Say, "If you love Allah, then follow me and Allah will love you and forgive you for your wrong actions. Allah is Ever-Forgiving, Most Merciful." (Surah Al 'Imran: 31)**

As mentioned in the verse above, if we want Allah to love us, we need to comply with that to which our Prophet, may Allah bless him and grant him peace, calls us and meticulously practise it.

# MIRACLES OF THE QUR'AN

We mentioned earlier that the greatest miracle given to our Prophet, may Allah bless him and grant him peace, is the Qur'an. The Qur'an was sent to mankind 1,400 years ago, but there are some facts related in the Qur'an whose meanings we have only been able to uncover recently.

From the planets to the stars, human beings to animals, Allah created everything in the universe. Our Lord already

knows everything we have not discovered so far and He informs us about some of that in the Qur'an. We can only learn these things when Allah permits us, and then we realise that they are miracles of Allah.

The Qur'an contains many scientific miracles. Here, we will deal with only some of the scientific miracles of the Qur'an. (*For further information, you can refer to the book, Miracles of the Qur'an.*)

## How The Universe Came Into Existence

The origin of the universe is described in the Qur'an in the following verse and in many others:

**He created the heavens and the earth from nothing...**
**(Surat al-An'am: 101)**

In the first section of the book, we described in detail how the universe came into existence from nothing 15 billion years ago. In other words, the universe suddenly came into existence from nothing.

Only the science of the twentieth century enabled us to attain scientific evidence of this great event. Therefore, it was impossible to know this scientifically 1,400 years ago. But, as is also mentioned in the previous verse, Allah told us this fact when the Qur'an was first revealed. This is a miracle of the Qur'an and one of the pieces of evidence that it is the Speech of Allah.

He is the Originator of
the heavens and
the earth...

(Surat al-An'am: 101)

## Orbits

Many of you know that our world and the other planets have orbits. In fact, not only do the planets in our Solar System have orbits, but also all heavenly bodies in the universe have their separate orbits. That is, they all move in very precisely computed paths. This scientific truth that scientists have only recently uncovered was revealed 1,400 years ago:

**It is He Who created the night and the day, and the sun and the moon. They swim along, each in an orbit. (Surat al-Anbiya: 33)**

As is also seen in this verse, Allah informs us about a scientific fact which was only discovered recently. At the time the Qur'an was revealed, people did not know that heavenly bodies moved in constant orbits. But Allah knows everything and tells what He wills to His slaves.

## The Seas' Not Mingling With One Another

One of the properties of seas that has only recently been discovered is related in a verse of the Qur'an as follows:

**He has let loose the two seas, converging together, with a barrier between them they do not break through. (Surat ar-Rahman: 19-20)**

This property of the seas, that they come together yet do not mingle with one another at all, has only very recently been discovered by oceanographers. Because of the physical force called "surface tension," the waters of neighbouring seas do not mix. Caused by the difference in the density of their waters, surface tension prevents them from mingling with one another, just as if a thin wall were between them.

The interesting side to this is that during a period when people had no knowledge of physics, surface tension or oceanography; this was revealed in the Qur'an.

## The Roundness of the Earth

The understanding of astronomy of the time, when the Qur'an was revealed, perceived the world differently. It was then thought by some that the earth was flat, and others had different theories. But the fact that the earth was round was not then generally known. However, from the Qur'an it was understood by implication that the shape of the world is round. The relevant verse reads:

**He has created the Heavens and the Earth for Truth. He wraps the night up in the day, and wraps the day up in the night... (Surat az-Zumar: 5)**

The Arabic word *"takwir"* is translated as "to wrap" in the above verse. In English it means "to make one thing lap over another, folded up as a garment that is laid away." The day and the night wrapping over each other can be true only if the earth is round. But, as mentioned above, the Arabs who lived 1,400 years ago thought that the earth was flat. This means that the roundness of the world was hinted at in the Qur'an, which was revealed in the seventh century. That is because Allah teaches the truth to mankind. This matter, indicated in the Book revealed by Allah, was verified only centuries later by scientists.

Since the Qur'an is Allah's word, the most correct words were used in it when describing the universe. It is unlikely that a human could know and choose these words. But because Allah knows everything, He can make these facts available to man at any time He wills.

## Fingerprints

While it is stated in the Qur'an that it is easy for Allah to bring man back to life after death, Allah draws attention in particular to peoples' fingertips:

**Does man imagine We will not reassemble his bones?**

**Yes, We are able to put together in perfect order the very tips of his fingers. (Surat al-Qiyama: 3-4)**

Bringing an utterly decayed human body back to life is

very easy for Allah. Now, examine your fingertips. Everyone's finger-prints are unique to himself. If you had a twin, his/her fingerprints would also be different. Every person who is alive or who has ever lived in this world has a unique set of fingerprints. That is why they are almost as unique as the identity of a person.

Allah the Almighty can re-create us, down to all these fine details. Meanwhile, we need to keep in mind that the significance of fingerprints and that the fact that every person has a set of fingerprints peculiar to himself was only discovered in the nineteenth century. But Allah drew attention to the tips of the fingers 1,400 years ago in the Qur'an.

There are several other issues miraculously indicated by the Qur'an. We have only discussed a few of them here. These alone suffice to make clear that the Qur'an is the Speech of Allah. (For further information, you can refer to the book, *Miracles of the Qur'an by Harun Yahya*.)

Allah informs us the following about the Qur'an:

**Will they not ponder the Qur'an? If it had been from other than Allah, they would have found many inconsistencies in it. (Surat an-Nisa: 82)**

As is also evident from the verse above, the Qur'an provides accurate information. With advances in science, more of the miracles mentioned in the Qur'an are being revealed. These miraculous attributes of the Qur'an prove that it is a revelation from Allah. At this point, it is our job to learn and practise the commands of the Qur'an meticulously.

Allah commands us to adhere to the Qur'an in many verses. Some of them are as follows:

**And this is a Book We have sent down and blessed, so follow it and do your duty so that hopefully you will gain mercy. (Surat al-An'am: 155)**

**…Truly it is a reminder, and whoever wills pays heed to it. (Surah 'Abasa: 11-12)**

# WHAT KIND OF A CHARACTER DOES ALLAH DEMAND FROM US?

The Qur'an, which is a guide to all humanity, is the Speech of Allah. We can attain the character that will please Allah by reading the verses of the Qur'an and living by them. This is really easy. But despite this, some people make the mistake of drifting away from the values that please Allah. If one day, everyone around you complied with Allah's wishes and embodied the values Allah demands from man, then this world would become a much better place. Now let's see briefly what these qualities are.

We all know that Allah created man. Consequently, Allah best knows the good and wicked qualities man possesses. A person may well deceive other people, but he can never hide anything from Allah. That is because, unlike us, Allah knows man's inner thoughts. Therefore, a person must always be sincere and honest towards Allah. One verse reads:

> **Say, "Whether you conceal what is in your breasts or make it known, Allah knows it. He knows what is in the heavens and what is on earth. Allah has power over all things." (Surah Al 'Imran: 29)**

> **Everything in the heavens and everything in the earth belongs to Allah. Whether you divulge what is in yourselves or keep it hidden, Allah will still call you to account for it. He forgives whomever He wills and He punishes whomever He wills. Allah has power over all things. (Surat al-Baqara: 284)**

A person who is aware that Allah hears every word he utters, knows each act he does and every thought that crosses his mind, would never dare to engage in a wicked act, even if it were hidden from other people. This means that, to be truly good, people must absolutely believe in Allah's existence and His unity, acknowledge His might and be aware that He sees and hears everything. This is one of the prerequisites of attaining the values Allah demands from His slaves.

## Loving Allah and Putting One's Trust in Him

You cherish the love your parents show you, do you not? You also love them. They protect and love you and meet your needs. You trust them. If you encounter a difficulty, you know they are always there to help you.

Have you ever thought how much you love Allah and trust Him?

Allah meets all the needs of all the beings He creates. Thanks to His infinite mercy, we live in this world in peace and enjoy countless blessings.

Allah created the sun so that we can live on earth. Allah also created vegetables, fruit and animals for us. We have bread, milk, meat and various other delicious vegetables and fruit because Allah creates them all for us.

114

Allah created rain so that we can have fresh water to drink. He created oceans, the continuous bodies of salt water. Without rain there would be neither fresh nor salt water on earth. Water is vital for us. As you know, man can only survive without water for a few days.

Allah placed the immune system within our bodies to protect us against microbes. Thanks to our immune systems, we do not die from the simple microbe that causes the common cold.

Aside from these matters, Allah makes our hearts beat unceasingly throughout our lives. If our hearts needed rest at certain intervals, as do engines, we would certainly die. But hearts beat unceasingly for decades without rest and enable us to live.

Allah created eyes to see, ears to hear, noses to smell and tongues to taste. These are only a few of the blessings Allah has given us. We cannot count all the blessings Allah gives us. In one verse, Allah, Who is very merciful to us, addresses us as follows:

**He has given you everything you have asked Him for. If you tried to number Allah's blessings, you could never count them. Man is indeed wrongdoing, ungrateful. (Surah Ibrahim: 34)**

As you have also understood from the Qur'an, being ungrateful for these blessings, forgetting that all blessings are from Allah and not thanking Him for everything He has done for us, is wicked behaviour. Allah does not love those who are ungrateful.

In return for His blessings, Allah only wants us to love Him, and to be grateful to Him, that is, to thank Him. His command is related in the verse as follows:

**Allah brought you out of your mothers' wombs knowing nothing at all, and gave you hearing, sight and hearts so that perhaps you would show thanks. (Surat an-Nahl: 78)**

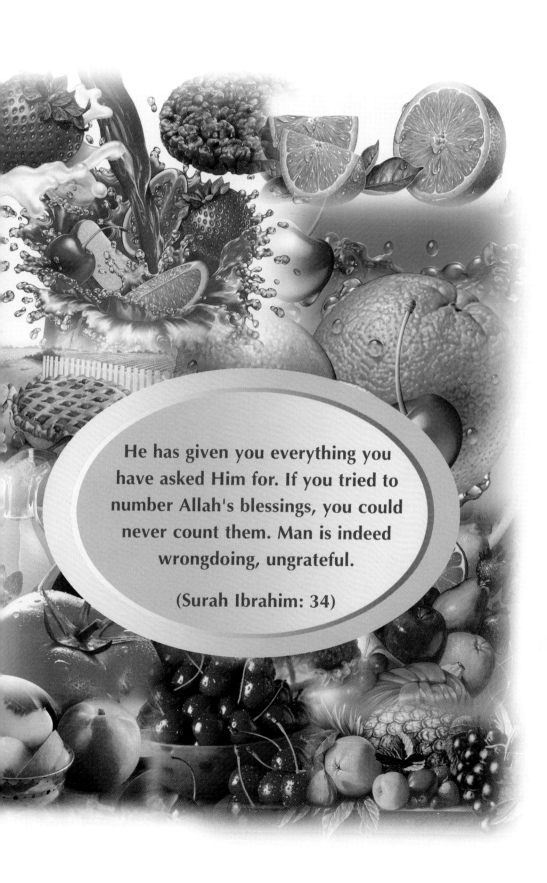

He has given you everything you have asked Him for. If you tried to number Allah's blessings, you could never count them. Man is indeed wrongdoing, ungrateful.

(Surah Ibrahim: 34)

So eat from what Allah has provided for you, lawful and good, and be thankful for the blessing of Allah if it is Him you worship. (Surat an-Nahl: 114)

It is He who has created hearing, sight and hearts for you. What little thanks you show! (Surat al-Muminun: 78)

In another verse, it is related that those who have faith love Allah most:

Some people set up equals to Allah, loving them as they should love Allah. But those who have faith have greater love for Allah. If only you could see those who do wrong at the time when they see the punishment, and that truly all strength belongs to Allah, and that Allah is severe in punishment. (Surat al-Baqara: 165)

Allah brought you out of your mothers' wombs knowing nothing at all, and gave you hearing, sight and hearts so that perhaps you would show thanks.

(Surat an-Nahl: 78)

Allah protects and nourishes your mother, father and everyone else. We are all in need of Allah. Neither our parents nor we could have possibly done these things. For this reason, we must love Allah and put our trust in Him.

Loving Allah more than anyone or anything else, putting trust in Him and acknowledging that He has given us everything are the foremost qualities of character with which Allah is pleased.

# How Must We Conduct Ourselves Towards Other People?

Allah prohibits people from being arrogant, lying, mocking others and being proud. Being honest and modest are traits with which Allah is pleased.

Some people often live under the influence of people around them. If they have wicked friends, they may be negatively influenced by them. But a person who believes in Allah and acknowledges that He constantly sees him never swerves from right action, no matter how compelling the conditions may be. He becomes a good example to those who are dishonest and prone to mischief.

Allah loves steadfast people. The term "steadfastness" in the Qur'an is not limited to being steadfast in the face of ordeals, but means being steadfast at every moment of one's life. The steadfastness of a person who has faith does not change according to people or events. For instance, a person with little fear of Allah may be good to someone from whom he expects to derive benefit, but fail to demonstrate this praiseworthy attitude consistently. Once he feels his interests are at stake, he may abruptly change. A person of faith, however, meticulously avoids misconduct. He responds to everyone with excellent manners and is committed to keep doing so, no matter what the conditions are or what people's attitudes may be. Even though he is enraged, he manages to control himself and shows steadfastness.

In one verse, Allah commands people to compete in being steadfast:

**You who believe, be steadfast; be supreme in steadfast-ness; and remain stationed; and have fear of Allah; so that hopefully you will be successful. (Surah Al 'Imran: 200)**

The steadfastness of the prophets mentioned in the Qur'an sets an example for us. As you will remember, the suffering of Ayyub, peace be upon him, lasted a very long time. But this

noble slave of Allah showed steadfastness and prayed to Allah. Allah answered his prayer and showed him a way out.

Nuh, peace be upon him, displayed steadfastness when people mocked him because of the Ark he built. He remained calm and counselled them. These are the extraordinary examples of steadfastness displayed by these noble people. Allah relates in many verses that He loves His slaves who are steadfast.

Allah, on the contrary, does not love arrogant people who show off. Not all people enjoy the same material benefits in this world. Some have beautiful houses and cars while others may possess nothing, but what matters is that one conducts oneself correctly. For instance, assuming that one is superior to one's friends because one has better clothes is an attitude that displeases Allah. That is because Allah commands us to value people according to their faith, not their appearances.

For Allah, the measure of superiority is not wealth or might, beauty or strength. Allah values people according to their taqwa (awe of Allah), the love they feel for Him, their loyalty and their commitment to living by the values of the Qur'an. These are the criteria for assessing superiority in Allah's sight. In the Qur'an, Allah relates the story of Qarun to teach us a lesson.

Qarun was a very wealthy man. He was so rich that the keys to his treasure had to be carried by several people. Ignorant people around him yearned to be like Qarun and wished they had everything he had. But Qarun was an arrogant and boastful person who was not obedient to Allah. He denied that Allah had given him all his wealth. So, Allah inflicted a terrible disaster on Qarun: He and all his possessions disappeared in one single night. Upon this terrible disaster, those who yearned to be like him expressed their joy at not being in his place. They all recognised that this was a punishment from Allah.

Qarun is mentioned as an example in the Qur'an as follows:

**Qarun was a very rich and arrogant person.**

Qarun was one of the people of Musa but he lorded it over them. We gave him treasures, the keys alone to which were a heavy weight for a party of strong men. When his people said to him, "Do not gloat. Allah does not love people who gloat." (Surat al-Qasas: 76)

He went out among his people in his finery. Those who desired the life of the world said, "Oh! If only we had the same as Qarun has been given! What immense good fortune he possesses."

But those who had been given knowledge said, "Woe to you! Allah's reward is better for those who have faith and act rightly. But only the steadfast will obtain it."

We caused the earth to swallow up both him and his house. There was no group to come to his aid, besides Allah, and he was not someone who is helped.

Those who had longed to take his place the day before woke up saying, "Allah expands the provision of any of His slaves He wills or restricts it. If Allah had not shown great kindness to us, we would have been swallowed up as well. Ah! Truly the disbelievers are not successful." (Surat al-Qasas: 79-82)

The Qur'an informs us that "gossiping" and "backbiting" are some of the other behavioural traits disliked by Allah. Spying on someone's mistakes, backbiting and making a person a target for mockery are behaviour that a person who fears Allah must studiously avoid. In the Qur'an Allah forbids gossiping and backbiting. The relevant verse reads:

> **You who have faith! Avoid most suspicion. Indeed some suspicion is a crime. And do not spy and do not back-bite one another. Would any of you like to eat his brother's dead flesh? No, you would hate it. And have fear of**

**Allah. Allah is Ever-Returning, Most Merciful. (Surat al-Hujurat: 12)**

As is also evident from the verse, Allah tells us in the Qur'an that backbiting is as disgusting as eating one's dead brother's flesh.

Allah tells us to conduct ourselves correctly in the course of our daily lives. Life is an opportunity granted by our Lord to follow His right path. Today, most people are unaware of this. Instead of complying with Allah's commands and advice, they seek other guides. Being influenced by the films they watch or the songs to which they listen, they adopt erroneous values. For instance, young people who watch a merciless and cruel hero in a movie often start to imitate him right after they leave the theatre.

A wise and sincere person, however, always displays the character traits with which Allah is pleased. The prophets are the people in whose footsteps we must follow. The character traits we must have are those values with which Allah is pleased. These include being merciful, forgiving, modest, humble, steadfast and obedient to Allah and His Messenger. A person who adopts these noble values does not stoop to becoming involved in disputes; He rather settles them and shows tolerance. Instead of being rebellious and disobedient to one's parents, the Qur'an commands us to be obedient and respectful. In the Qur'an, Allah stresses the importance of being respectful towards one's parents:

128

**Your Lord has decreed that you should worship none but Him, and that you should show kindness to your parents. Whether one or both of them reach old age with you, do not say "Ugh!" to them out of irritation and do not be harsh with them but speak to them with gentleness and generosity.**

**Take them under your wing, out of mercy, with due humility and say: "Lord, show mercy to them as they did in looking after me when I was small." (Surat al-Isra: 23-24)**

Being obedient towards one's parents, not showing the slightest sign of irritation to them by saying "Ugh," and always

being merciful and tender-hearted towards them are important character traits Allah demands from us. Showing these traits will both earn us Allah's love and make us more happy and peaceful in our daily lives.

One can only display these character traits praised in the Qur'an when one lives by Islam. Disbelieving people can hardly be committed to embodying these noble values. You must avoid being like these people and always keep in mind the verse that reads: **"Or did you imagine that you were going to enter the Garden without Allah knowing those among you who had struggled and knowing the steadfast?" (Surah Al 'Imran: 142)** Never forget that Allah will love you more and grant more of His blessings to you when you are steadfast, humble, self-sacrificing, generous, and when you conduct yourself correctly.

# WORSHIP ALLAH

O ur Lord, the Creator of everything within you and around you, possesses infinite might. Allah created us and commands us to obey Him and to conduct ourselves correctly as described in the Qur'an. Everything our Lord demands from us is worship. Fasting, praying, being grateful to Allah, being steadfast, and engaging in good deeds are a few of these acts of worship.

But the majority of people, despite being aware of their responsibilities, do not want to accept this. Because of their sinful arrogance they find it difficult to be obedient to Allah. They do not want to listen to Allah's words since they consider themselves very important. Declining to accept that Allah created them, they dare to rebel against Him. Although it is Allah Who gave them their hearts, ears, their health, and, in brief, everything on this earth, they do not feel grateful to Him for all these favours.

But these people will feel great regret. Being ungrateful and arrogant will cost them a troublesome life in this world and deep regret in the hereafter. The ingratitude *(kufr)* they display in this world will entail the fires of Hell.

Every person who does not want to suffer regret and be one of those who will enter the Fire must be grateful to Allah. Allah wants us to be grateful to Him and to pray and to worship Him in return for all the blessings He has given us. So, when you see these beautiful and perfect blessings surrounding you—which could never have come into existence by them-selves—you must remember Allah and feel thankful to Him. Do not be one of those who fail to notice and appreciate any of the blessings they are given.

In the Qur'an, Allah commands us to practice forms of worship other than feel-ing grateful to Him. Performing the prayer five times a day, fasting during the month of Ramadan, paying the zakat (wealth tax) and making the hajj (making the pilgrim-

age to Makkah once in a lifetime) if one is able are other forms of worship Allah demands from us.

Praying five times a day and establishing the prayer in our lives, in our families and in our communities help us regularly to remember our weaknesses as slaves before Allah. It is an act of worship to be fulfilled at certain times. Allah informs us in the Qur'an that this form of worship helps us abstain from the wicked deeds with which Allah is displeased.

Fasting is also a form of worship commanded in the Qur'an. During the month of Ramadan, Allah demands that we not eat and drink in the daytime. Fulfilling this worship, we show steadfastness while going without food and drink for a certain period of time.

Paying the zakat, on the other hand, is giving a portion of one's wealth to the poor and needy and others who may receive it. As with other forms of worship, fulfilling this is very important because avoidance of meanness, and showing self-sacrifice are character traits that please Allah. This aside, paying the zakat improves co-operation between people and matures the human spirit.

# Supplication is a Way to Draw Closer to Allah

Allah attaches great importance to supplication. Allah relates the importance of supplication in the verse stating: **"Say: 'What has My Lord to do with you if you do not call on Him? ....' "** **(Surat al-Furqan: 77)** As this verse suggests, a person's value before Allah depends on his prayer. That is because a person who prays asks for what he needs from Allah alone. Allah is the Owner of everything.

Allah creates everything we need. Take, for example, the food that is essential for human life. Allah creates vegetables, fruit, chickens, cows and so on. Allah creates your parents and all the people around you. Allah, the All-Mighty, endows people with the bodies, intelligence, knowledge, strength, health and the opportunities they enjoy.

As mentioned earlier, Allah creates all these as blessings for us. We owe the food we eat to Allah. Similarly, we owe the ability to eat this food to Allah. Think of this for a moment! How would you be able to chew your food without your teeth? How would you digest it without your stomach? Would the existence of food have any meaning if we did not have digestive systems?

You are nourished by Allah's will. Because it is Allah Who gives all blessings to us, it is Allah to Whom we must pray when we want something to happen or to obtain something.

Consequently, we must ask for everything from our Lord.

An example will allow you to understand this matter better:

You press a button to turn on the light. Can you say that the button creates the light? Of course, you cannot. The button is only a means, as are the cables transmitting the electricity. In this world, Allah creates causes for every effect. He created water. In dams this water is run through massive turbines, and so electricity is produced. Cables transmit electricity and finally the bulb transforms electricity into light. But the fact is that it is

Allah Who creates light. If Allah willed it, He could create electricity without these causes. But our Lord wants us to use our intelligence, to think, to consider what Allah has created and, in this way, to come to faith.

You turn the tap on when you want water. But can you say that it is the pipes or the tap that cause water to come into existence? Just as in the case of the button, the tap is only a means, not the cause.

This is the outlook we must adopt, and it also explains why we need to pray to Allah. That is because Allah creates everything.

A list of reasons why we need to thank Allah and pray to Him would fill millions of volumes of books. That is why the existence of people around you who do not attach importance to these must never dissuade you. Their failure to employ their intelligence and their avoidance of thought and reflection draw them into great error.

Allah informs us of the end awaiting these people. Our reward or punishment in the hereafter depends on how we conduct ourselves in this world and whether we strive to draw closer to Allah. Every person will be recompensed for his deeds in the hereafter.

### - How Can We Supplicate?

Thinking of Allah's might and grandeur, feeling awe of Him and praying humbly and secretly are essential for supplication. Allah informs us how to pray in the Qur'an.

**Call on your Lord humbly and secretly. He does not love those who overstep the limits. (Surat al-A'raf: 55)**

Supplication cannot be limited to certain places or time. We can think of Allah and pray to Him at any moment. Allah commands as follows in the Qur'an:

**Those who remember Allah, standing, sitting and lying on their sides, and reflect on the creation of the heavens and the earth: "Our Lord, You have not created this for nothing. Glory be to You! So safeguard us from the punishment of the Fire." (Surah Al 'Imran: 191)**

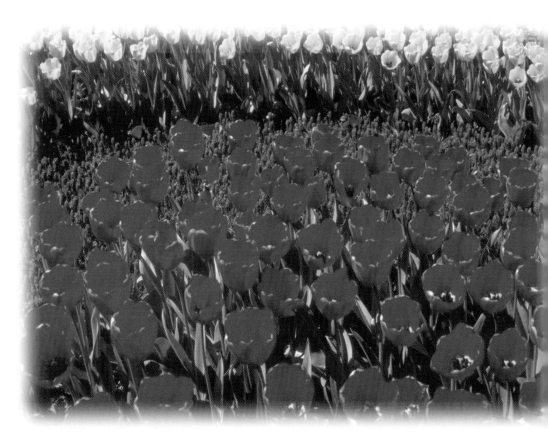

**Remember Me—I will remember you. Give thanks to Me and do not be ungrateful. You who have faith! Seek help in steadfastness and prayer. Allah is with the steadfast. (Surat al-Baqara: 152-153)**

Allah provides us with examples of supplications in the Qur'an. Some of the prayers of the prophets and believers are related as follows:

**He [i.e., Nuh] said, "My Lord, I seek refuge with You from asking You for anything about which I have no**

knowledge. If You do not forgive me and have mercy on me, I will be among the lost." (Surah Hud: 47)

And when Ibrahim built the foundations of the House with Isma'il: "Our Lord, accept this from us! You are the All-Hearing, the All-Knowing. Our Lord, make us both Muslims submitted to You, and our descendants a Muslim community submitted to You. Show us our rites of worship and turn towards us. You are the Ever-Returning, the Most Merciful. Our Lord, raise up among them a Messenger from them to recite Your Signs to them and teach them the Book and Wisdom and purify them. You are the Almighty, the All-Wise." (Surat al-Baqara: 127-129)

[Yusuf said:] "My Lord, You have granted power to me on earth and taught me the true meaning of events. Originator of the heavens and earth, You are my Friend in this world and the Next. So take me as a Muslim at my death and join me to the people who are true." (Surah Yusuf: 101)

[Sulayman said:] "...My Lord, keep me thankful for the blessing You have bestowed on me and on my parents, and keep me acting rightly, pleasing You, and

admit me, by Your mercy, among Your slaves who are true." (Surat an-Naml: 19)

Say, "O Allah! Master of the Kingdom! You give sovereignty to whomever You will You take sovereignty from whomever You will. You exalt whomever You will You abase whomever You will. All good is in Your hands. You have power over all things." (Surah Al 'Imran: 26)

He [i.e., Musa] said, "O Lord, expand my breast for me and make my task easy for me Loosen the knot in my tongue so that they will understand my words. Assign me a helper from my family, my brother Harun. Strengthen my back by him and let him share in my task, so that we can glorify You much and remember You much, for You are watching us." (Surah Ta Ha: 25-35)

143

Those who remember Allah, standing, sitting and lying on their sides, and reflect on the creation of the heavens and the earth: "Our Lord, You have not created this for nothing. Glory be to You! So safeguard us from the punishment of the Fire. Our Lord, those You cast into the Fire, You have indeed disgraced. The wrongdoers will have no helpers. Our Lord, we heard a caller calling us to faith: 'Have faith in your Lord!' and we had faith. Our Lord, forgive us our wrong actions, erase our bad actions from us and take us back to You with those who are truly good. Our Lord, give us what You promised us through Your Messengers, and do not disgrace us on the Day of Rising. You do not break Your promise."

Their Lord responds to them: "I will not let the deeds of any doer among you go to waste, male or female—you are both the same in that respect..." (Surah Al 'Imran: 191-195)

# DEATH AND THE LIFE OF THE HEREAFTER

Some people consider death as the ultimate end. But the truth is that death is a transition from the life of this world to the life of the hereafter. It is like a gate to the afterlife.

On the other side of this gate, that is, in the life of the hereafter, whether we will attain the Garden or the Fire depends on our pure belief in Allah's unity and Allah's approval of our deeds and conduct here in this world.

Death is only the end of a certain period of time. This is similar to the ringing of bell at school signalling the end of an examination. Allah has granted a different period of trial to each man. Some have thirty years, while some others enjoy a life as long as one hundred years. Just as Allah decided your date of

146

birth, which is the beginning of your time of examination, Allah decides the time when this period will end. In other words, only Allah knows at which age you will die.

## How should we consider death?

Death, that is, the end of the period of examination in this world, is a source of happiness and joy for believers. One would hardly feel sorry for someone who has successfully passed an examination, would one? Feeling grief over someone who dies is likewise ridiculous. It may well be that you have lost a close relative or someone you love. But a person of faith acknowledges that death is certainly not a permanent separation, and that someone who dies merely finishes his period of examination in this world. He knows that in the hereafter, Allah will gather Muslims who live by His commands together and reward them with the Garden. In this case, rather than being sorry, people will feel great happiness.

Allah can take our souls at any moment. Therefore, we ought to strive to earn Allah's good pleasure.

To conclude, death is not an end but a gate leading us to the hereafter. The life of the hereafter is the real life that will last for all eternity, and we need to prepare for it. Do you think that a person who takes an examination wants it to last forever? Of course not. He only wants to answer the questions correctly and leave the classroom.

In this world, too, a man must strive to pass his examination, earn Allah's good pleasure and attain His Garden.

In this world, the most important goal of man must be to love Allah and to earn His good pleasure. That is because, our Lord, the All-Merciful, loves us and protects us at every moment. One verse of Qur'an, quoting the words of one of the prophets, reads:

**"...My Lord is the Preserver of everything." (Surah Hud: 57)**

## The Hereafter

Allah describes the temporary nature of this world in many verses of the Qur'an and stresses that the real abode of man is in the hereafter. A man who is tested in this world will one day be overtaken by death and thus start his life in the hereafter. This is life without end. In his eternal life, the soul of man will not disappear. Allah creates countless blessings in this world. He created the life of this world to see how we will conduct ourselves in return for the blessings we enjoy. As a reward or punishment, Allah has also created the Garden and the Fire.

Allah informs us how a person will be repaid in His presence in the hereafter:

**Those who produce a good action will receive ten like it. But those who produce a bad action will only be**

**repaid with its equivalent and they will not be wronged. (Surat al-An'am: 160)**

Allah is very merciful towards people. He rewards them generously. But those who deserve punishment are only repaid with the equivalent of their wicked deeds. Allah does not wrong anyone. People may treat one another unjustly. In this world, a guilty person may deceive or mislead others, but in the hereafter if he does not believe in Allah and in His unity, Allah will certainly punish him, and if he is a Muslim Allah may punish or forgive him. Allah sees and knows everything, and thus repays every deed.

## The Garden and the Fire

The Garden and the Fire are the two separate places where people will spend their lives after death. It is again the Qur'an that provides us accurate information about these places.

You might have been to places with beautiful landscapes or seen breathtaking scenes in movies. There may be places you wished you had never left. The Garden is incomparably more beautiful than any of these places. The food believers will enjoy in the Garden is much more delicious than the food of this world.

Allah, the Creator of all beauty in this world, informs us that He creates much greater beauty in the Garden for sincere believers.

## Trouble in This World Makes Us Understand Better the Beauty of the Garden

We suffer various troubles in this world. We become sick, we may break arms or legs, we feel very cold or hot, our stomachs become upset, our skins become bruised, etc. Look at your parents' photographs in their youth and think about their faces today. You will notice the difference.

Allah specially creates such weaknesses for man in this world. None of them exist in the hereafter. Once weaknesses in this world are reflected upon, we can better appreciate the worth of the Garden. Attaining the Garden erases all these troubles. Think about what displeases you in this world…None of it exists in the hereafter.

The Garden is decorated with the blessings from which man takes most pleasure. The best of what we eat and drink in this world have their flawless counterparts in the Garden. Man never feels cold or hot in the Garden. He never becomes sick, fears, grieves or grows old. You cannot find a single wicked man there. That is because wicked people, those who disbelieve in Allah and deny Him, remain in the Fire, a place they deserve. People in the Garden speak graciously with one another; they do not curse, become angry, shout or hurt others. All the good people who have a real belief in the unity of Allah and who act in such a way as to please Allah and thus deserve the Garden will be there, residing as friends forever.

From the Qur'an we know that magnificent things exist in the Garden: Splendid mansions, shady gardens and flowing rivers add to the joy of people of the Garden. In fact, what we have outlined above is truly insufficient to describe the blessings of the Garden. The beauty of the Garden is beyond even our imagination.

In the Qur'an, Allah informs us that in the Garden, man will attain more of what he expects. Think of something you want to have or somewhere you want to travel. By Allah's will, you will have them in a single moment. In one verse Allah states the following:

**...You will have there everything you demand. (Surah Fussilat: 31)**

Some of the verses in the Qur'an that relate the beauty of the Garden are as follows:

**An image of the Garden which is promised to the right-eous: in it there are rivers of water which will never spoil and rivers of milk whose taste will never change and rivers of wine, delightful to all who drink it, and rivers of honey of undiluted purity; in it they will have fruit of every kind and forgiveness from their Lord... (Surah Muhammad: 15)**

As for those who believe and do right actions—We impose on no self any more than it can bear—they are the Companions of the Garden, remaining in it timelessly, for ever.
(Surat al-A'raf: 42)

As for those who believe and do right actions, We will lodge them in lofty chambers in the Garden, with rivers flowing under them, remaining in them timelessly, forever. How excellent is the reward of those who act.

(Surat al-Anqabut: 58)

...You will have there everything
you demand.

(Surah Fussilat: 31)

As for those who have faith and do right actions, We will lodge them in lofty chambers in the Garden, with rivers flowing under them, remaining in them timelessly, for ever. How excellent is the reward of those who act. (Surat Al-'Ankabut: 58)

They will enter Gardens of Eden where they will be adorned with gold bracelets and pearls, and where their clothing will be of silk. (Surah Fatir: 33)

The Companions of the Garden are busy enjoying themselves today, they and their wives reclining on couches in the shade. They will have fruits there and whatever they request. (Surah Ya Sin: 55-57)

Amid thornless lote-trees and fruit-laden acacias and wide-spreading shade and outpouring water and fruits in abundance never failing, unrestricted. And on elevated couches. (Surat al-Waqi'a: 28-34)

Allah also informs us that the people who deserve the Garden will remain there for all eternity:

As for those who have faith and do right actions—We impose on no self any more than it can bear—they are the

**Companions of the Garden, remaining in it timelessly, for ever. (Surat al-A'raf: 42)**

Essentially, a believer takes pleasure from attaining the good pleasure of Allah. Knowing and feeling this is the greatest joy one can ever have in this world.

Amid thornless lote-trees
and fruit-laden acacias and
wide-spreading shade and outpouring
water and fruits in abundance
never failing, unrestricted.

(Surat al-Waqi'a: 28-33)

## The Torment in the Fire

People who rebel against Allah and refuse to accept His existence will also be repaid for what they did. They did not accept Allah or believe that He is the One Who creates everything, and they showed arrogance, failed to perform the acts of worship expected of them and thus they rebelled in this world. In return for all these, they will be punished in the Fire.

Some people commit various crimes in this world. In situations where no one sees them, they may also go unpunished. But these people fail to acknowledge that Allah sees them every moment, and that He knows even their inner thoughts.

Everyone will be repaid for the good or bad acts they perform. Allah has infinite justice, and in the verses of the Qur'an He gives the glad tidings that even the tiniest good deed will be bountifully rewarded. Allah also informs us that people will be rewarded if they repent and ask for forgiveness from Him. Nevertheless, Allah threatens people who do not believe in Him, fail to comply with the commands in the Qur'an and think that no life exists after death.

The Fire is the reward of the guilty and those who do wrong by rebelling against Allah. Allah describes the situation of these people in the Qur'an as follows:

**Those who took their religion as a diversion and a**

**game, and were deluded by the life of the world. Today We will forget them just as they forgot the encounter of this Day and denied Our Signs. (Surat al-A'raf: 51)**

In the Fire a grievous punishment, which is not comparable with any pain in this world, awaits the people of the Fire. The Fire is a place abounding with fear, pain, desperation and unhappiness. The people of the Fire pray to Allah and ask for a way out of the Fire. But once in the Fire, it is too late to feel sorrow or regret. We mentioned to you earlier about the regret Pharaoh felt. Allah grants man opportunities until the moment of his death. Once he dies and starts his life in the hereafter, however, feeling regret is no longer of any use.

The people of the Fire live a life infinitely worse than that of animals. The only nourishment they have is the fruit of the bitter thorn and the tree of Zaqqum. Their drink is blood and pus. With skin rent, flesh burned, and blood splattering all over, they lead a degrading life. Hands tied to their necks, they are cast into the core of fire. Furthermore, this life of suffering lasts for all eternity, unless Allah wills otherwise.

Allah, states the following in the Qur'an:

**Above them is a sealed vault of Fire. (Surat al-Balad: 20)**

**That is because they say, "The Fire will only touch us for a number of days." Their inventions have deluded them in their religion. (Surah Al 'Imran: 24)**

However, what a Muslim person who knows his own errors and wrong actions must do is regret them, pray and seek Allah's forgiveness. In the Qur'an, Allah informs us that He will forgive any wrong action provided that we sincerely repent. The relevant verse reads as follows:

**Say: "My slaves, you who have transgressed against yourselves, do not despair of the mercy of Allah. Truly Allah forgives all wrong actions. He is the Ever-Forgiving, the Most Merciful." (Surat az-Zumar: 53)**

It is important for a person to know his own errors and ask for forgiveness from Allah in order to avoid regret in the here-after, and to save himself from the unbearable torment of the Fire.

# CONCLUSION

Dear Children! In this book we have dealt with the most fundamental and important facts about our lives. We asked questions such as, "What is the purpose of our lives?," " How does our Lord, Who created us and everything surrounding us, want us to conduct ourselves?," " What are our responsibilities towards our Creator?," "What is the life of the Hereafter?," "Why should we fear being sent to the Fire?," etc.

We hope you think about these questions very carefully. Right now, you are very young, but never forget that one day you will also be an old man or woman.

There may be people around you who will tell you that you are too young to think about death. But you must keep in mind that no one knows when death will come upon him or her. You may encounter death in a day or in ten years' time. When you think about all these things, you will immediately realise how senseless it is to waste time.

Never forget that you can always make up an excuse for everything. You can even convince other people. But in the life in the hereafter which is due to begin upon death, you will not be able to make any excuses for your faults and wrongdoings in the presence of Allah, Who knows and sees everything.

For this reason, you must think about these facts without losing time and begin striving to become a person who is loved by Allah.

---

*…"Glory be to You!*
*We have no knowledge except what You have taught us.*
*You are the All-Knowing, the All-Wise."*
*(Surat al-Baqara: 32)*

Many people think that Darwin's Theory of Evolution is a proven fact. Contrary to this conventional wisdom, recent developments in science completely disprove the theory. The only reason Darwinism is still foisted on people by means of a worldwide propaganda campaign lies in the ideological aspects of the theory.
This book clarifies the scientific collapse of the theory of evolution in a way that is detailed but easy to understand. It reveals the frauds and distortions committed by evolutionists to "prove" evolution. Finally it analyzes the powers and motives that strive to keep this theory alive and make people believe in it.
238 PAGES WITH 166 PICTURES IN COLOUR

One of the purposes why the Qur'an was revealed is to summon people to think about creation and its works. When a person examines his own body or any other living thing in nature, the world or the whole universe, in it he sees a great design, art, plan and intelligence. All this is evidence proving Allah's being, unit, and eternal power.
*For Men of Understanding* was written to make the reader see and realise some of the evidence of creation in nature. Many living miracles are revealed in the book with hundreds of pictures and brief explanations.
288 PAGES WITH 467 PICTURES IN COLOUR

This book gives an insight into some good moral aspects of the Karma philosophy which are in agreement with the Qur'an, as well as its twisted views which conflict with human reason and conscience. The book also explains why following Allah's way and living by the Qur'an is the only way to real happiness, peace, and security.

Many societies that rebelled against the will of God or regarded His messengers as enemies were wiped off the face of the earth completely...
*Perished Nations* examines these penalties as revealed in the verses of the Quran and in light of archaeological discoveries. This book is also available in German, French, Spanish, Russian and Portuguese.
149 PAGES WITH 73 PICTURES IN COLOUR

In a body that is made up of atoms, you breathe in air, eat food, and drink liquids that are all composed of atoms. Everything you see is nothing but the result of the collision of electrons of atoms with photons.
In this book, the implausibility of the spontaneous formation of an atom, the building-block of everything, living or non-living, is related and the flawless nature of Allah's creation is demonstrated.
139 PAGES WITH 122 PICTURES IN COLOUR

Forgetting that death is likely to put an end to this life at any time, man simply believes that he can enjoy a perfect and happy life. Yet he evidently deceives himself. The world is a temporary place specially created by Allah to test man. That is why, it is inherently flawed and far from satisfying man's endless needs and desires. This book explains this most important essence of life and leads man to ponder the real place to which he belongs, namely the Hereafter.
224 PAGES WITH 144 PICTURES IN COLOUR

Have you ever thought that you were non-existent before you were born and suddenly appeared on Earth? Have you ever thought that the peel of a banana, melon, watermelon or an orange each serve as a quality package preserving the fruit's odour and taste? Man is a being to which Allah has granted the faculty of thinking. Yet a majority of people fail to employ this faculty as they should... The purpose of this book is to summon people to think in the way they should and to guide them in their efforts to think.

128 PAGES WITH 137 PICTURES IN COLOUR

People who are oppressed, who are tortured to death, innocent babies, those who cannot afford even a loaf of bread, who must sleep in tents or even in streets in cold weather, those who are massacred just because they belong to a certain tribe, women, children, and old people who are expelled from their homes because of their religion... Eventually, there is only one solution to the injustice, chaos, terror, massacres, hunger, poverty, and oppression: the morals of the Qur'an.

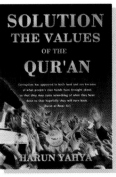

208 PAGES WITH 276 PICTURES IN COLOUR

Darwin said: "If it could be demonstrated that any complex organ existed, which could not possibly have been formed by numerous, successive, slight modifications, my theory would absolutely break down." When you read this book, you will see that Darwin's theory has absolutely broken down, just as he feared it would.

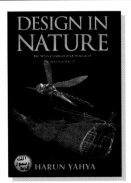

208 PAGES WITH 302 PICTURES IN COLOUR

In the Qur'an, there is an explicit reference to the "second coming of the Jesus to the world" which is heralded in a hadith. The realisation of some information revealed in the Qur'an about Jesus can only be possible by Jesus' second coming...

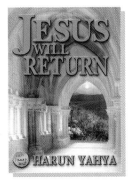

102 PAGES

Colours, patterns, spots even lines of each living being existing in nature have a meaning. For some species, colours serve as a communication tool; for others, they are a warning against enemies. Whatever the case, these colours are essential for the well-being of living beings. An attentive eye would immediately recognise that not only the living beings, but also everything in nature are just as they should be. Furthermore, he would realise that everything is given to the service of man: the comforting blue colour of the sky, the colourful view of flowers, the bright green trees and meadows, the moon and stars illuminating the world in pitch darkness together with innumerable beauties surrounding man...

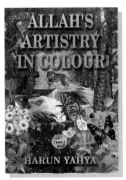

160 PAGES WITH 215 PICTURES IN COLOUR

Never plead ignorance of Allah's evident existence, that everything was created by Allah, that everything you own was given to you by Allah for your subsistence, that you will not stay so long in this world, of the reality of death, that the Qur'an is the Book of truth, that you will give account for your deeds, of the voice of your conscience that always invites you to righteousness, of the existence of the hereafter and the day of account, that hell is the eternal home of severe punishment, and of the reality of fate.

112 PAGES WITH 74 PICTURES IN COLOUR

# CHILDREN'S BOOKS

This book examines the activities people engage in and the events they experience every day, from the point of view of Muslims who live by Qur'anic values. The aim is to reveal the pleasing lives of believers thanks to the morality of the Qur'an, and to call everyone to that morality, which offers a superior life.

Have you ever thought about the vast dimensions of the universe we live in? As you read this book, you will see that our universe and all the living things therein are created in the most perfect way by our Creator, Allah. You will learn that Allah created the sun, the moon, our world, in short, everything in the universe so that we may live in it in the most peaceful and happy way.

Dear children, while reading this book, you will see how Allah has created all the creatures in the most beautiful way and how every one of them shows us His endless beauty, power and knowledge.

Countless species live on the earth, some of which you will be familiar with, and others not. Each one of these creatures, from the dogs or cats which you come across every day, to the wild animals living in the jungle, have wonderful features and fascinating abilities. All of these are a reflection of Allah's infinite power and artistry. In this book, you will read about the interesting features and amazing accomplishments of these wonderful creatures.

Children! Have you ever asked yourself questions like these: How did our earth come into existence? How did the moon and sun come into being? Where were you before you were born? How did oceans, trees, animals appear on earth? Who was the first human being? Your mom gave birth to you. Yet the first human being could not have had parents. So, how did he come into existence?" In this book you will find the true answers to these questions. The book is also available in Serbo-Croat and Indonesian.